The Beginning Teacher's Handbook For Elementary School

Lori Friesen

The Beginning Teacher's Handbook for Elementary School

Library and Archives Canada Cataloguing in Publication

Friesen, Lori
The beginning teacher's handbook for elementary school / Lori Friesen.

Includes bibliographical references.
ISBN 978-1-55059-352-5

1. Elementary school teaching. 2. Classroom management.
3. Motivation in education. I. Title.

LB1555.F74 2008 372.1102 C2008-901308-5

Detselig Enterprises Ltd.
210, 1220 Kensington Road NW
Calgary, Alberta
T2N 3P5

DETSELIG
ENTERPRISES LTD

www.temerondetselig.com
temeron@telusplanet.net
Phone: (403) 283-0900
Fax: (403) 283-6947

We acknowledge the support of the Government of Canada through the Book Publishing Industry Development Program (BPIDP) for our publishing program.

We also acknowledge the support of the Alberta Foundation for the Arts for our publishing program.

Alberta Foundation for the Arts
Alberta
COMMUNITY DEVELOPMENT
COMMITTED TO THE DEVELOPMENT OF CULTURE AND THE ARTS

SAN 113-0234
ISBN 978-1-55059-352-5
Cover Design by Alvin Choong

This book is dedicated with love to
my parents, who were my very first teachers,
to my little brother, who was my very first student,
and to my patient and loving husband,
who continually grounds and inspires me.

This book is also dedicated to my students
who have taught me so much,
and to all of the beginning teachers
who are fortunate enough to have found this calling.

Contents

Welcome!

Dear Beginning Teacher,

Congratulations on choosing a *wonderful* career. There is nothing more rewarding or fulfilling than teaching children. This next year will be unlike any you have ever experienced; you will laugh, you will cry, and you will be incredibly challenged. However, you are probably feeling a little bit scared and overwhelmed right now; this is completely natural. Even experienced teachers feel this way from time to time. You are not alone!

The purpose of this handbook is to help guide you through times like these. To truly be there for children and their needs, YOU need to be organized and prepared in advance. Therefore, I have included checklists to help to get you on the right track at the beginning of the year. You will also find a wealth of ideas, strategies, and activities that work and come from experienced teachers to use throughout the year. However, please do not feel that you have to do everything suggested in this handbook! Be gentle with yourself – the biggest problem that we seem to have as beginning teachers is trying to do too much in our first year. Only select ideas that match your personal teaching style and context, and do them well.

I was once a beginning teacher myself; this, combined with my experiences working with preservice teachers both in my own classroom and in the university setting, has helped me to develop a thorough understanding of the needs of beginning teachers. One of the best pieces of advice I can offer you is to remember to take time for yourself this year. You can only remain enthusiastic for students if you maintain a life outside of the classroom. Be proactive and keep your stress levels to a minimum by scheduling time for yourself.

I hope that this handbook will make your first year successful and enjoyable!

Sincerely,

Lori Friesen

Lori Friesen

INTRODUCTION

WHAT THE RESEARCH TELLS US

It was a moment I will never forget. The idealism and excitement I felt was overwhelming. Twenty-five years old, just having returned from a two year overseas teaching and travelling adventure in Australia, New Zealand, Hong Kong, South East Asia and Japan, I was now being offered my first teaching assignment in Canada. I walked out of the room and with every step, my panic rose. Where was I to begin?

I was soon to discover that my situation as a beginning teacher was not unique. "Life for beginning teachers has traditionally been described as a sink-or-swim proposition" (Ingersoll & Smith, 2003, p.33), whereby the new teacher is simply told: "There's your classroom. Here's your book. Good luck" (Johnson & Kardos, 2002, p. 13). In a study by Henke, Chen, & Geis in 2000, it was discovered that "one in five new teachers will leave the profession within 3 years of entry." Further, a longitudinal interview study of 50 new teachers by Johnson & Birkeland in 2003 found that 80% of the teachers who chose to leave the profession in their study "…left because they were overwhelmed by the demands of the job and saw few prospects for improvement or success." Teaching is one of the few professions which "makes the same demands on novices as it does on experienced practitioners" (Black, 2004, p.47); we fail to recognize that "beginning teachers have legitimate learning needs that cannot be grasped in advance or outside the contexts of teaching" (Feiman-Nemser, 2003, p. 26). However well prepared and committed they may be, "beginning teachers have no assurance that they will succeed in the classroom because teaching, by its very nature, is unpredictable work" (Johnson & Birkeland, p.26).

This knowledge became the motivation behind my decision to design a handbook to help beginning teachers of elementary students get ready for their very first teaching assignment. My main concern at that time, as a beginning teacher, was that I did not know what I needed to do to make my first year successful. Knowledge of practical techniques and ideas from experienced teachers would have made a world of difference. Most importantly, I learned very quickly that although I had chosen this profession because I truly loved children, I was often not able to give the students my full attention. This was because I was continually pre-occupied with other matters which could have been dealt with beforehand, if I only had the foresight and knowledge to do so. This is a common experience for beginning teachers. In Johnson and Birkeland's 2003 study, one beginning teacher stated that "despite his graduate training, Derek felt unprepared for the classroom, lacking the 'bag of tricks or the firm foundation' that a veteran would have"" (p.596).

Many districts have responded to this call for support with the development of mentoring programs for beginning teachers. A close, supportive relationship with a veteran teacher is invaluable to a beginning teacher, but this type of a relationship is not always possible for a number of reasons. Because of the demands of the profession, many mentors "do not have enough time to engage in discussions about the pressing, school-specific questions of curriculum, instruction, and classroom management that most concerned (beginning teachers)" (Johnson & Kardos, 2002). One novice teacher commented that "although the teachers at (the) school are friendly, they rarely work together and do not provide (her) with the kind of advice and support she looked for: They weren't there when I needed them" (Johnson & Birkeland, 2003, p. 599). Although some of the 50 teachers interviewed in Johnson & Birkeland's study in 1999 worked in schools where novices received organized support from experienced teachers, many respondents were simply left alone as they learned how to teach (Kardos, Johnson, Peske, Kauffman, & Liu, 2001).

The numerous problems that first-year teachers face, as perceived by beginning teachers, are well documented in the research. The table on the next page attests to the variety of different issues that have been identified. Almost certainly, the number one problem for first-year teachers is that of *classroom management and discipline* (Dollase, 1992; Housego & Badali, 1996; Nielbrand, Horn, & Holmes, 1992; Veenman, 1984). This occurs "despite the likely emphasis on management during the practicum and some preparation in university course work" (Housego & Badali, 1996). Romana and Gibson (2006) also found that "since the pivotal work on beginning teacher concerns by Veenman (1984), little has been done to further investigate what novice teachers are experiencing for the purposes of understanding how their concerns might be met during their first year;" however, "classroom management remains an important area for teacher education programs." Continued difficulties with classroom management are reflected in current articles and studies focused on beginning teacher experiences: Black, 2004; Feiman-Nemser, 2003; Frieberg, 2002; Johnson & Kardos, 2002; Renard, 2003; Romano & Gibson, 2006; Sargent, 2003. This should be of great concern to administrators, colleagues, and parents of students, because when beginning teachers are anxious about their classroom management skills, "management difficulties undermine (their) sense of effectiveness" (Feiman-Nemser, 2003, p. 28) in the classroom.

Problems Facing First-Year Teachers

Problems of the First-Year Teacher	Study the Promblem was Cited In
Confusion about personal teaching style.	C. Nielbrand, E. Horne, & R. Holmes (1992).
Confusion about theory and practice.	C. Nielbrand, E. Horne, & R. Holmes (1992).
Content and pedagogy.	Romano & Gibson (2006).
Day to day operational difficulties in the school environment (inconsistent operations/structure).	Johnson & Birkeland (2003).
Effectiveness with students.	Johnson & Birkeland (2003).
Evaluation of curriculum materials.	R.H. Dollase (1992); B.E.L. Housego & S.J. Badali (1996).
External policy.	Romano & Gibson (2006)
Fear of asking for help, appearing inadequate.	K. Tellez (1992); Johnson & Kardos (2002).
Feelings of helplessness and loneliness; overwhelmed by job demands.	K. Merseth (1992); Johnson & Birkeland (2003).
Heavy workload and job stress.	R. H. Dollase (1992); Johnson & Birkeland (2003).
Inadequate teaching materials and/or curriculum resources.	C. Nielbrand, E. Horne, & R. Holmes (1992); Johnson & Birkeland (2003).
Mismatch with mentor teachers.	K. Telez (1992), Johnson & Kardos (2002).
Morality questions, i.e. students cheating.	R. H. Dollase (1994).
Non-supportive administration and colleagues.	H. Dollase (1992); C. Nielbrand, E. Horne, & R. Holmes (1992); Johnson & Birkeland (2003).
Not being accepted as a 'real' teacher.	R. H. Dollase (1994).
Organization of class work.	C. Nielbrand, E. Horne, & R. Holmes (1992).
Overwhelming paperwork.	F. O'Connell Rust (1994).
Personal issues.	Romano & Gibson (2006).
Planning of lessons.	R. H. Dollase (1992).
Problems of individual students; inclusion and special needs students.	S. Veenman (1984); C. Nielbrand, E. Horne & R. Holmes (1992); Gibson & Romano (2006).
Relations with students.	R. H. Dollase (1992).
Teacher evaluation.	Johnson & Birkeland (2003); Romano & Gibson (2006)
Teacher having difficulty seeing themselves as an authority figure.	R. H. Dollase (1994).

After classroom management/discipline, the four most common problems experienced by beginning teachers as indicated in the research are: Student motivation, dealing with individual differences between students, assessment tasks, and ability to develop effective relationships with parents (Britton, Paine, & Raizen, 1999; Dollase, 1992; Housego & Badali, 1996; Nielbrand et al., 1992; O'Connell Rust, 1994; Veenman, 1984). Veenman (1984) found that motivation of students ranked the second highest in the list of perceived problems, and "dealing with individual differences among students was the third most frequently mentioned problem" (p.156). Struggles with Inclusion and special needs students as well as involving parents effectively in the classroom are featured in Gibson and Romano's 2006 study of 50 beginning teachers. Housego & Badali (1996) note that "another area of difficulty . . . was assessment, which was also one of the topics beginning Newfoundland and American teachers highlighted as needing attention" (p.364). Other problems commonly expressed by first-year teachers are outlined in the chart on the next page (in no particular order) alongside the studies in which they were cited. When noted in more than one study, both are listed.

Although "some things can only be learned when teachers have their own classrooms, additional teaching experiences during the preparation program could be provided to better prepare preservice teachers for practice" (Romano & Gibson, 2006). Research evidence suggests that the more training prospective teachers receive, the more likely they are to stay; "graduates of extended five-year programs also report higher levels of satisfaction with their preparation and receive higher ratings from principals and colleagues" (Darling-Hammond, 2003, p. 10). Beginning teachers turn to many different types of resources to help ensure successful teaching, such as other teachers in the school, school administration, and their own family. Books are another type of support for beginning teachers (Romano & Gibson, 2006, p. 12), particularly when a positive mentor relationship is not established or possible. It is my hope that this resource will provide you, the beginning teacher, with the support you need to make your first year positive and fulfilling.

Acknowledgements

This book would not have been possible without the contributions and support of many of my teaching colleagues and friends. I would especially like to thank the following people.

Dr. Robin Bright, my life-long mentor and inspiration.

Lorraine Wolsey, whose passion, energy, and support is unparalleled.

Elizabeth Nevels, whose friendship and advice is golden.

Anita Grant, an unexpected gift in my teaching landscape.

And to the teachers and administration of Mike Mountain Horse Elementary School who supported and guided me though my first year.

With sincere thanks and admiration.

CHAPTER 1: THE COUNTDOWN BEGINS!

CHECKLISTS OF TO-DO'S BEFORE SCHOOL STARTS

A love of children and the desire to guide them to a higher level of knowledge intellectually, socially, and emotionally. It is the driving force behind why we have chosen this profession. Yet to be effective, we need to be organized and therefore prepared to meet children's needs. During my first year of teaching, I learned quickly that this is a fundamental quality in a dynamic, effective teacher. To truly be there for children with their hundreds of curious questions and 'guess what?' stories, we need to be well-organized. Therefore, I have designed five checklists for you to help keep track of what you need to do (if possible!) prior to that first day.

INSTRUCTIONAL SUPPLIES

Your school may have many of the supplies listed here. Please modify this list as you deem necessary for your grade level and instructional situation:

- ☐ grade book, with dividers for specific subject areas
- ☐ blank CD's and/or disks
- ☐ attendance book
- ☐ note paper
- ☐ blank white paper
- ☐ pens and pencils
- ☐ markers
- ☐ crayons
- ☐ chalk and chalk holder
- ☐ chalkboard erasers
- ☐ ruler(s) – a class set if possible

- ☐ metre sticks
- ☐ scissors
- ☐ paper clips
- ☐ stapler and staples
- ☐ thumbtacks
- ☐ tape
- ☐ mac-tak
- ☐ construction paper
- ☐ other arts and crafts materials
- ☐ late/absence notes
- ☐ receipt book if money is to be collected
- ☐ first-name checklist of students to keep track of returned field trip forms, money for special activities, lunch money, etc.

- ☐ reference books
- ☐ maps
- ☐ charts
- ☐ globe
- ☐ number line
- ☐ alphabet (manuscript display or cursive)
- ☐ manipulatives for math and science activities
- ☐ sets of texts or instructional materials for each content area
- ☐ accompanying teacher guides for these texts
- ☐ curriculum guides for your grade level
- ☐ books for your classroom library

- ☐ whiteboard
- ☐ whiteboard markers and eraser
- ☐ bulletin board paper
- ☐ bulletin board borders
- ☐ laminated letters for bulletin boards
- ☐ overhead projector
- ☐ TV and/or VCR (or find out where and how to access these)
- ☐ library/media resources
- ☐ educational games/free time activities
- ☐ pencil sharpeners that work (and an electric one if possible)
- ☐ trash cans

- ☐ clock
- ☐ timer
- ☐ cleaning supplies (paper towels, rags to clean up spills, all-purpose cleaner, dust pan and brush)
- ☐ party supplies (napkins, cups, drink crystals, plastic plates, cutlery)

- ☐ My shopping list:

  ____
  ____
  ____
  ____
  ____
  ____
  ____
  ____
  ____
  ____

Classroom Environment

Frieberg (2002) is correct to note that "often, (beginning teachers) are not taught how to establish the positive, organized learning environments necessary for them to teach and for students to learn" (p. 56) in teacher preparation programs. However, children and parents gain a very lasting first impression when they walk into your classroom. Your objective should be to let the children know immediately that they are loved and cared for, and that they belong in this room. Do you have a welcome sign on the door of your classroom? On my door I've made several huge flowers in bright colors with each child's name and picture on their own petal. The title above the flowers says "Love Grows Here." It may seem like such a simple thing but welcoming students in this ways sends a clear message that they belong and are cared for. When children enter the classroom they should be able to see their names in at least 5 places, regardless of the grade you are teaching. You can label the door when they first enter, their desks, their name-tags, where they will keep their jackets/shoes/lunch kits, where they will store their personal supplies, the helper board, etc. Upper elementary students need these 'warm fuzzies' just as much as students in lower grades! Your classroom needs to be a warm and welcoming place and a well-designed space to facilitate easy movement of students. What message are you sending to students and parents? Here are some things you will need to keep in mind when setting up your classroom:

Desk Arrangement:

- ☐ Organization of desks (rows, small groups, pairs, u-shape).
- ☐ Location of teacher's desk. Be sure that you can easily monitor the classroom while at your desk, and remain physically close to your students as this will help to minimize discipline problems.
- ☐ Location of filing cabinet(s).
- ☐ Determine seating chart or allow student choice for seating.
- ☐ Be sure to accommodate for children with special needs with regard to your seating plan, i.e. vision, hearing impaired, learning disability.
- ☐ Be sure all students are able to comfortably see the board and/or projection screen from where they are sitting.
- ☐ Ensure students can move easily between desks/furniture.

★ I recommend keeping the students in the traditional, straight rows for at least the first week of school. Although it may not sound like your teaching style, it may help to minimize Behavior problems and give you an opportunity to understand how the children interact before making any permanent decisions about seating arrangement. Further, it is important to change the seating arrangement every month or every two months. This encourages children to get to know everyone in their classroom and facilitates moving children who may find it difficult to work together.

Furniture Arrangement:

Be sure consider the following question . . .

- ☐ Will you have a reading table for small group instruction?
- ☐ Will there be a calendar corner? I especially encourage this for younger children for calendar time, morning meeting activities, and for story time.
- ☐ If not, is there a space where the whole class can meet?
- ☐ Will you have a rug, cushions, stuffed animals, soft chairs, or a small couch in your calendar corner? (I have found garage sales to be a wonderful source for these items!)
- ☐ Where will your classroom library be? How will you organize/display books? Will your books be levelled for varying ability levels?
- ☐ Will you have a puppet theatre?
- ☐ Will you have a listening centre with a tape player, earphones, and recorded books?

- ☐ Do you have a computer in your classroom? If so, how will you keep track of who has used it? In my classroom, I have clothes pins attached to one side of my computer using a long piece of masking tape with student names on them; when students have had a turn at the computer, they put their clothes pin on the other side of the computer. Once everyone has had a turn, we put the clothes pins back on the left side randomly and begin again!
- ☐ Will you have a 'construction centre' with lego sets or other building materials appropriate to your grade level?
- ☐ Will you have an 'art area' with an easel and paints, or a crafts table?
- ☐ Will you have some plants in your room?
- ☐ An aquarium?
- ☐ Are the electrical outlets easily accessible with your chosen furniture arrangement?
- ☐ Where will you store your overhead projector?
- ☐ Have you tested all equipment to ensure it works before you intend to use it?

General Classroom Organization:

- ☐ Where will your students hand in their work? In/out baskets work well and are inexpensive to buy, beg, and borrow!
- ☐ Where will your students store their personal belongings (coats, hats, shoes, lunches, etc.)?
- ☐ Have you set aside storage space for students' supplies? (Shelves, filing cabinets, tote trays, cans, or manila envelopes in a basket all will do the trick!)
- ☐ Have you prepared a class list and posted it outside your door along with your name?
- ☐ Have you made or bought a welcome sign and put it on the door?

Bulletin Boards

Start early on this one – it takes longer than you think! Here are some possible topics:

- ☐ Announcements and school information
- ☐ Calendar and current events
- ☐ Classroom/school rules
- ☐ Emergency/fire drill procedures

- ☐ Student work display. A nice way to keep this as a permanent display all through the year is to make a checkerboard pattern using two different colors of construction paper across your bulletin board, and label each square with a child's name. This way, any time that you or the student wishes to display a piece of work, the space is available!
- ☐ Birthday chart with students' names on it. One great idea that will help you to stay organized for birthday celebrations all year is to label one paper bag for each child in your class and place a small gift (or gifts) inside. Then staple each paper bag to a colorful birthday celebration bulletin board. You can then invite each child to take his or her gift off of the bulletin board on their special day!
- ☐ Classroom 'helpers' chart (this will be discussed in more detail in Chapter 2)
- ☐ Daily/weekly schedule
- ☐ Student of the week
- ☐ Quote of the week
- ☐ Word of the week
- ☐ Word wall
- ☐ Fall (and other seasons later)
- ☐ Guess who? (student baby pictures)
- ☐ Safety (walking to/from school, school bus etc.)
- ☐ Things done over the summer (photos)
- ☐ Student-created bulletin board by project or topic/theme
- ☐ "Bookworm." Put up the head in September, and then have students add a paper plate for each new book they read throughout the year, recording their name, the title of the book, and their rating (from 1-10) on each plate.

The Students

Students are the reason that we are all here. Now that you have all of the materials, and you have set up your classroom for success, let's meet the students (prior to the first day!)

- ☐ Obtain a class list.
- ☐ Include a copy of students' addresses, phone numbers, and birthdays in your grade book (and record birthdays on your wall chart).
- ☐ Record the name of the parent/guardian for each child.
- ☐ Keep the emergency contact for each child in an easy access location.

You may wish to look at the students cumulative files for the following information on your students. However, I feel that a word of caution is necessary here. Try to remain objective. Be careful to not form opinions about children prior to getting to know them.

- ☐ Look at student pictures and do your best to learn children's names before the first day.
- ☐ Learn about students' family/home life situation.
- ☐ Pay attention to information about student health status and/or allergies.
- ☐ Check to see which children were previously involved in any special needs programs.
- ☐ Consider outstanding strengths or weaknesses, interests, and capabilities, both academic and non-academic
- ☐ Is there a larger than expected number of high or low achievers? Will grade level texts be appropriate?
- ☐ Talk with children's former teachers if you have specific concerns.
- ☐ Prepare a file folder for each child in which to keep samples of their work, diagnostic tests, and other information.
- ☐ Make name cards for students to wear on the first day.
- ☐ Put names on desks with mac tak (or have students make them and choose where they will be sitting).
- ☐ Prepare a package to go home with students on the first day, including:
  - ☐ A welcome newsletter (please see samples in the Appendix).
  - ☐ Forms required by the school.
  - ☐ Classroom timetable, including library exchange date.
  - ☐ Explanation of homework assignments.
  - ☐ Information regarding your Home Reading Program (if applicable).
  - ☐ Supply list.
  - ☐ Calendar of upcoming special events/field trips and/or school calendar.
  - ☐ Alternatively, you may decide to send a letter home BEFORE school starts, either to the parents or to each student.
  - ☐ Or, visit the home of each student before the beginning of school.

The Staff

Building strong relationships with the people you will be working with can be your lifeline to help you through your first year of teaching. Sometimes just knowing that there are people who you can talk to when you've had 'one of those days', or when you have questions about the school or your teaching, co-workers can be the boost that you need if and when you are feeling overwhelmed. Here are some of the people I would strongly encourage you to get to know early on in the year:

Other Teachers

Take the time to:

- ✓ Find out where their rooms are.
- ✓ Ask lots of questions!!! (Please do not be afraid to do this.)
- ✓ Go out for lunch together sometime before school starts in the fall.
- ✓ Have coffee together.

Mentor

A mentor can be a wonderful working relationship during your first year.

- ✓ Find out if your school has a mentoring program.
- ✓ Seek out how to become involved in this program.

Teacher Aides

- ✓ Find out if you have an aid assigned to your room.
- ✓ Determine which child is (s)he assigned to work with.
- ✓ Ask if (s)he has worked with this child before.
- ✓ If so, ask if (s)he has any suggestions or strategies that have worked well with this child in particular.
- ✓ Find out his/her schedule.

Grade Level or School Specialists

Who is your grade level's or the school's:

- ☐ Secretary: ______________________________
- ☐ Librarian: ______________________________
- ☐ Caretaker: ______________________________
- ☐ Nurse: ______________________________
- ☐ Counsellor: ______________________________

- ☐ Speech Therapist: ____________________
- ☐ Media Specialist: ____________________
- ☐ Early Literacy Specialist: ____________________
- ☐ ESL teacher: ____________________
- ☐ Gym Teacher: ____________________
- ☐ Art Teacher: ____________________
- ☐ Music/Band Teacher: ____________________
- ☐ Bus Drivers: ____________________

The School Policies and Procedures

Each school is different and the policies and regulations within each school reflect this. Take some time to become familiar with how your school is run prior to the first day so that you can reduce stress when you begin teaching. Ask your principal, the secretary, your mentor, or other teachers as many questions as you can! Get a school map and become familiar with where rooms for special classes will be (i.e. music, speech therapy, gym, early literacy/remedial reading specialist, etc.). Your school should also have a handbook and a school calendar (ask your principal) which may answer many of these questions:

- ☐ Which curriculum resources are available for my use?
- ☐ Who do I ask for keys to my classroom/the school?
- ☐ How do I get materials and supplies?
- ☐ How do I order materials I need?
- ☐ What photocopying equipment is available, and what is the policy for its use?
- ☐ How can I get furniture I need in my classroom?
- ☐ Do you have a schedule for students who attend special classes?
- ☐ When are my gym, music, art, computer, and library classes scheduled?
- ☐ What are the school rules I will need to present to my students?
- ☐ When is Meet the Teacher Night?
- ☐ Where are the student cumulative files, and what is the policy regarding their use?
- ☐ When are staff meetings?
- ☐ What are the principal's requirements for lesson plans?
- ☐ What audiovisual materials and equipment are available, and what is the procedure for checking them out?
- ☐ What is the office phone use policy?

- ☐ Where is the lost and found?
- ☐ Is there a policy on room parties?
- ☐ What is the policy on field trips?
- ☐ Do classroom helpers need to check in at the office?
- ☐ What are my responsibilities for playground duty?
- ☐ What are my responsibilities for lunchroom duty?
- ☐ Is there a lunch program? If so, how is it run?
- ☐ Do I have any bus students in my classroom?
- ☐ Do bus students leave my classroom several minutes early?
- ☐ Where do they meet?
- ☐ Am I responsible for supervising bus loading/unloading?
- ☐ Does our school have an assembly procedures?
- ☐ Are there any assemblies during the first week(s) of school that I should be aware of?
- ☐ What is the fire drill procedure?
- ☐ How do I attain a copy of the report card I'll be using?
- ☐ What is the grading system I'll be using?
- ☐ How will my students be tested?
- ☐ When are report cards issued?
- ☐ When are parent/teacher interviews?
- ☐ Is the building open on evenings and weekends?
- ☐ What do you expect from me as my principal?

School District Policies and Procedures:

Your district will have a handbook which will answer all of your questions regarding contacts, curriculum, payroll, and benefits. Ask your principal for a copy of this handbook.

CHAPTER 2: THE FIRST DAY OF SCHOOL!

TIPS FOR THE FIRST DAY

It is natural to feel nervous about your first day of teaching, but know that you are not alone. Almost every new teacher, and even many veteran teachers, have told me that they feel this way. Here are some tips to help you to prepare for that very first day:

- ✓ Maintain a positive attitude.
- ✓ Plan everything for you and your students to the minute.
- ✓ Plan extra activities.
- ✓ Choose activities for the first day that allow the children many small successes.
- ✓ Remember to be flexible.
- ✓ *Enjoy Yourself!* This is going to be fun!

A great way to start your first day is to greet your students at the door and then show them to their seat or have them choose a seat for themselves. Involve the children in a short, interesting activity as everyone gets settled and while you attend to the many administrative duties associated with the first day of school. The children could do one of the following:

- ☆ Open goodie bags or explore tubs filled with lego, markers/crayons and paper, finger puppets, books, beads and string, math manipulatives, or puzzles.
- ☆ A summer fun word search (Appendix, page a.10).
- ☆ A crossword puzzle.
- ☆ A coloring activity set up at their desks.
- ☆ A 'find-someone-who' activity (Appendix, pages a.19-a.20).
- ☆ An interest inventory (Appendix, page a.11).
- ☆ Make their own name tags.
- ☆ Your own ideas: ______________________________

Once everyone has arrived and is settled, gather the children together in a large group (in a reading corner or other comfortable area) and share some information about yourself. For example, I have done quite a bit of travelling, so one of the things I like to do first is to pull down a map of the world, show the students the various countries I have been to, and then show them something special that I brought back from that country or tell them a story about what happened to me there. They love learning about their teacher and it's a lot of fun for me too! This will invite stories from many of your students about their own experiences and help to establish a warm climate in your classroom. Stories are a wonderful way to build relationships from the very beginning of the year.

Class Rules

When the students are feeling more comfortable with you (and you with them), it's a great opportunity for you to share the class rules with your students or have them generate a list of class rules with your guidance. I've done this both ways and the success of this strategy seems to depend on the group of children. Some classes come up with great rules (better than I could have), whereas other classes require more leadership in developing rules. I have found the following advice to be very useful when developing rules for your classroom:

- ✓ Choose only three to five rules at most.
- ✓ Keep language positive when stating rules.
- ✓ Ensure rules are appropriate to the child's developmental level.
- ✓ Teach, model, and practice each rule as carefully as you would any other lesson you teach.
- ✓ In addition to teaching your rules, ensure that you communicate clearly which positive rewards will be earned through following the rules and which consequences will be given if a child chooses to break a rule.

Many beginning teachers struggle with aspects of classroom management. This is partly because they may not realize that "classroom management is more than discipline. It involves, among other things, the development of classroom rules and rational consequences for breaking them" (Frieberg, 2002, p. 58). I have listed some examples on the next page of Behavior rules and policies that teachers have found successful at various grade levels. However, you will need to tailor your rules to your own teaching style.

Examples of Simple Class Rules For
Kindergarten to Grade Three Classes

1. Follow directions.
2. Only walking allowed.
3. Use good manners.
4. Listen to the speaker. Not only the teacher!
5. Raise your hand to speak.
6. Clean up after yourself.
7. Return materials when you are finished using them.
8. Leave toys at home.
9. Be ready to work.
10. Be kind to each other and to yourself.
11. Respect yourself and others.
12. Keep hands and feet to yourself.

Examples of Simple Class Rules
For Grade Four to Grade Six Classes

1. Have materials ready at the beginning of class.
2. Be on time.
3. Follow directions.
4. Ask for permission to leave the classroom.
5. Use appropriate language.
6. Listen to the speaker.
7. Leave hats at home.
8. Dress appropriately. Discuss in detail what this means.
9. Complete all homework on time.
10. Clean up after yourself.
11. Respect classroom and school property.
12. Treat others as you would like to be treated.

Routines

Getting off to a great start means knowing exactly what you will be expecting of your students and stating your expectations in a clear and positive manner. Be sure to think through routines for your classroom in advance and teach your expectations to your class within the very first week, focusing on several routines each day as they are needed. It is essential that you do not simply tell your students what your routines are but model and practice them until they become natural for your students in the classroom context. When teaching most routines, I follow this method:

1. **Teacher Model:** I first model the Behavior I expect of the students while the students observe. The students have opportunities to ask plenty of questions if needed at this point.
2. **Practice:** Next, we either practice the routine together as a class or, depending on the routine, I ask several volunteers to model it for us.
3. **Show Me:** Finally, I ask the students to model the Behavior for me as a class to see if they've 'got it'. I repeat these three steps for many of the routines several times during the first several weeks of school, and this saves me from having to continually remind students of my expectations throughout the year. Is important to remember that children will be children – some students will continue to test you throughout the year, regardless of how carefully you have taught these rules.

I have listed below some classroom routines you may want to consider using in your own classroom.

Classroom Routines:

The routines you choose and the jobs you may ask your students to do to contribute to your classroom community will depend on your own teaching style and what feels comfortable to you in the classroom. It is important to remember that "the new teacher who observes a master teacher's classroom in the middle of the year often misses the advance work and classroom management strategies that the master teacher used during the first few weeks of school to set the tone for a positive learning environment" (Frieberg, 2002, p. 57). Having clearly defined rules, routines, and expectations does not mean that you are not a 'fun' teacher - it means that you are well organized and have thought carefully about the emotional and physical safety of your students. Because my students understand that they are in a fair and predictable environment, I can engage them in activities not otherwise possible. The experiences students seem to remember most – special class cooking projects, mini field trips to other parts of the school property, and incredibly messy (and worthwhile) art projects – would not have been possible without these expectations and routines in place in advance.

☆ **Attendance**: What will your students be doing first thing in the morning and when they come into your classroom just after lunch while you are taking attendance? In my classroom, I use a whiteboard to print a special "Morning Message" in the same place each morning. This message is appropriate to the students' instructional level and is designed to specifically incorporate words that we are currently studying in our classroom that week. For example, the morning message might be:

> Frid_ _, February 29, 2008
>
> Do you kn_ _ why tod_ _ is a spec_ _l day?

I removed the letters "ay" twice in this message, because this is the spelling pattern we are currently working on. I have also deleted letters in "know" and "special" because these are two words I have noticed are often misspelled in my students' writing.

When the students come in in the morning, their "Morning Message" books are on their desks and they are to do their very best to fill in all of the missing spaces. After about 10 minutes (during which I have had a chance to take attendance, collect Scholastic book money, etc.), I go through the message with the class, asking for volunteers to help me to fill in the blanks. I use a different colour of marker to fill in the blanks so that students are able to see where we have added letters. We then read through the message together and talk about it. This is not intended to be busy work but, rather, a meaningful form of communication between myself and the students to begin our day. Variations on this activity include writing a sentence with three errors that the students need to find and correct, beginning with a joke of the day (but be careful here – some of the vocabulary might be very difficult for students to spell), or interspersing a morning language activity with a math question or problem-solving question. The possibilities are endless!

- ☆ **How to enter the classroom**: It may seem like common sense, but your expectations for how students are to enter the classroom need to be carefully modeled and taught in the first week of school. If you expect students to walk (not run) into the classroom and that they use quiet voices when they enter the classroom, it is unfair to expect students to know this without you explicitly telling them what your expectations are in this context. Students have a much better chance of being successful if you are clear about your expectations and state them positively.

- ☆ **Fire drill procedure**: Be sure to ask your principal prior to the first day of school about fire drill procedures. It is important to teach and practice your school's fire drill procedure with your class early, as soon as the second day of school if possible. Which door does your class need to go out of? Where should they assemble outdoors? Do the lights need to be turned off? Who does this? Does the classroom door need to be closed? Who is responsible for this job? These are all important safety procedures your students need to be familiar with.

- ☆ **Lock down procedure**: Lock down procedure is often practiced as a school due to the delicate nature of this event. Again, ask your school principal or other teachers at your grade level about this procedure prior to the first day of school if possible.

- ☆ **Use of playground equipment**: Who gets to use the playground equipment? There is often not enough equipment for every student. However, many little arguments about fairness can be easily dealt with by assigning the equipment for use by the boys on all even days and by the girls on all odd days.

- ☆ **Use of rest room and water fountain**: How will you keep track of who is out of the classroom using the rest room or getting a drink from the water fountain? In my classroom, I have each student's name on a magnet on the blackboard beside the door to our classroom (two sided magnetic tape works beautifully to make a magnet out of anything!). The rule in our classroom is that only one boy and one girl are allowed out of the room at any time. When students need to go to the rest room, they place their magnet under the word "Rest Room" on the blackboard as they leave the room, and then put it back when they return. This way I always know who is out of the classroom, especially should there be a fire drill or lock down procedure.

☆ **Use of pencil sharpener**: It took me awhile to figure out how much it drove me crazy to have a student begin sharpening his or her pencil when I was teaching a lesson, or how many students use the pencil sharpener as an avoidance strategy for getting to work! If you can afford it, I highly recommend purchasing an electric pencil sharpener for your room. What I did to eliminate pencil sharpening during class time was to label two empty coffee cans with "Sharp" and "Dull." I then appointed one student to be "Pencil Sharpener" on my job board (which changes each week). He or she would would sharpen pencils for 10 minutes each day at an established time. This way, whenever a student needs a sharp pencil, he/she simply returns the dull pencil for a sharp one!

☆ **Expected supplies**: It is important to remember that it is not always a student's fault in elementary school if he/she does not bring expected supplies. I always keep extra supplies on hand. I also have reminder notes to place in students' agendas to remind parents to please send whatever supplies are still needed. As part of my supply list, I ask students to bring one empty, clean, regular-sized coffee can with the child's name on it in which to store extra supplies. This minimizes clutter in students' desks and helps their supplies to last a little longer throughout the year!

☆ **Issuing of textbooks**: If your students will need to take textbooks home for homework assignments, it is important to have a clear, organized system for doing this. In my classroom, I numbered each of the textbooks and then assign a number to each student. This way, he/she is responsible for that textbook for the year, and it is easier to track a text should it go missing.

☆ **Work that is missed due to absences**: It can be tricky to keep track of work students have missed when they are sick. In my classroom, I keep a class set of manila envelopes in a cubby where students know they can find them. We have a "Nurse" job on my student job board. It is this student's responsibility to get the absent child's envelope and place it on his or her desk in the morning. Then, throughout the day as we complete assignments, the 'Nurse' places a copy of each assignment (if possible) into his or her envelope. When the absent child returns to school, the Nurse then takes care of telling the student about what he or she missed and answers questions as best as they can about the assignments. If the child who was absent still has questions, he or she then comes and asks me. I have found this to be a wonderful way for students to learn to take responsibility for each other, and it frees up some of my time as well!

- ☆ **Movement of students in room**: Again, if you expect students to walk when they are in the classroom (and this isn't clearly stated in your class rules), please ensure that you clearly state that this is your expectation.

- ☆ **Assign new students a student guide and recess buddy**: When we get a new student in our classroom it is always an exciting event! Students love to volunteer to be the "New Student Guide," and I have found this to be a wonderful way for students to begin to get to know each other and to feel a part of the group right away. This person is responsible for showing the new student around your classroom and school as well as answering their questions about rules and routines. It is also really important to ask who would like to volunteer to show the new student around at recess and lunch time so that he or she is not alone during these times.

- ☆ **What to do when finished work early**: Have you considered what you would like to invite the students to do when they are finished their work early? Two of the most popular activities in my classroom include what I call the "Mind Candy Centre" and the "Plasticine Station." I think that the success of the Mind Candy Centre is in part as a result of its' name – anything with the word *candy* in it seems to be a draw for children. However, what I did for this activity was use laminated pages from a wonderful book called *Teacher I'm Done: Now What Do I Do?* published by the Creative Teaching Press. This book includes activities such as letter and word puzzles, number puzzles, critical thinking/logic puzzles, and visual discrimination and creative thinking puzzles appropriate to each grade level. I place these activities in folders stapled to the "Mind Candy" bulletin board along with dry-erase markers and erasers. I am also sure to teach my expectations for the use of this centre. For the Plasticine Station, I have a large tub of odds and ends of different colors of Plasticine along with squares of wallpaper samples to protect students' desks (you can get these samples free from most wallpaper and paint stores!). The students are invited to take a chunk of Plasticine as big as the palm of their hand to play with at their desks. They love this activity!

- ☆ **Transitions between classes/subjects**: It is important to consider in advance what your expectations are for when students are transitioning to different classrooms and/or subjects within your room. Are students welcome to talk as much as they want? Are they free to get up and walk around for a bit? Do you have any expectations for volume level, or is this like a 'break' for the students? Like all of these routines, there is not a right or only way to do this. Your expectations will depend on your own teaching style; it is just very important that you are aware of what your expectations are so that you are not getting upset with students when you have not clearly communicated what you are comfortable with.

☆ **Name and date on assignments**: To save time throughout the year, I would recommend that you spend some quality time in the first few weeks teaching your students what you expect for name and/or date on assignments you do in class. Remember: model, teach, and practice this with your students, and continually praise them when they are doing well! This will save many questions throughout the year about "Do we have to put the full date on this?" or "Do we have to put our name at the top?" and so on.

☆ **Recording homework assignments:** In many schools now, students are given their very own agendas at the beginning of the year in which to write information such as homework assignments, field trip reminders, etc. each day. If you do not have these at your school, you can use a scribbler cut in half to serve this purpose as well. It is a wonderful way to keep in close contact with the parents of your students! Ensure that you set aside a particular time of the day that is the same each day so that it becomes a routine for your students. Right after lunch they know to come in and write in their agenda, just like in the mornings when my students come in and write their "Morning Message."

☆ **Conduct in the hallways**: Again, it is important to clearly communicate with students what your expectations are for walking in the hallway – before you leave the room! I always remind my students that I expect quiet voices (and of course, we talk about WHY this is important in the hallway) and "hands to yourself" so that bulletin board displays, student work, and any glass does not get disturbed on our travels. Before we leave the room, I will often tell my students that I am watching for a "Secret Star" who is following these rules. I select a student in my mind before we leave the room, and as we walk, I watch this secret student especially (but not obviously ☺). If, when we arrive at our destination, that student has done a great job following our hallway rules, our class is rewarded with a short 'chat break'. If the student didn't follow the rules, I do not tell the students who it was I was thinking of but that I hope we can try harder next time. This teaches students that there are times when we can be noisy and chatty, but that there are other times when we need to practice consideration for other students by keeping our voices to a minimum.

☆ **Playground conduct**: Often by mid-morning on the first day of school, my students are getting fidgety because they are used to their summer freedoms! This is a wonderful opportunity to take your class outside to teach and practice playground conduct. For example, at our school, we have three different soccer fields for recess. Each field is designated for two grades so that there are not grade one students being knocked over on the field by well-intending but much larger grade five students! Information such as this is very important for students to know, particularly when they are now in a new grade level. Our students also line up before coming back into the school at the end of recess (again, so little ones are not bowled over when they are trying to get back inside the school), so it is important that you take the time to find out for yourself and teach these small but important safety procedures to your new students.

☆ **Classroom schedule**: Again, students feel much more comfortable when they know that they are in a predictable, safe environment. When my students first come in in the morning, one of the first things they want to know is "What are we doing today?" My class schedule is posted on the wall in the form of a chart so that students always know what is happening on that day and what they can expect. As part of our morning routine, I will go through the schedule for that day to give a brief explanation of what we will be doing in each subject area.

☆ **End of the day duties**: We have many helper jobs in my classroom, which are described in the next section. In my classroom, we take the last fifteen minutes of each day to do our jobs once I have taught and modeled them. During the first week of school, I will usually teach the procedure for one new job each day.

Classroom Jobs

Class jobs may also be routines you want to consider using in your own classroom. I teach my expectations for class jobs in the same way that I teach my routines. The "Happy Helpers" bulletin board in my classroom is set up on a rotational basis and is changed each week, so students always know who is doing which job and which job they will be doing next. It is fun at the beginning of the year to enlist the help of your students as teachers; once one student has become an 'expert' at doing their job for the first week of school, (s)he can then teach the next student how to do the job successfully. Some examples of jobs you may wish to have students do daily are:

- ☐ Hand-out – 2 children (scribblers, texts, supplies).
- ☐ Pick-up – 2 children.
- ☐ Attendance (if you need to send it down to the office daily).
- ☐ Nurse (explained in previous section).
- ☐ Line Leader (for lower elementary grades).
- ☐ End of the Line.
- ☐ Water Plants.
- ☐ Lights (turns lights on and off).
- ☐ Sink (keeps the sink clean).
- ☐ Board Monitor (in charge of erasing and cleaning boards at the end of each day).
- ☐ Chairs – 2 children: In our school, the caretakers ask that we put all of the chairs up on the tables or desks at the end of the day.
- ☐ Librarian: In my classroom, this is the person in charge of keeping the library in order. He/she is also in charge of watching for other students who regularly put the books they are reading back where they belong. At the end of the week, he/she is in charge of rewarding those students with a small prize from me. This job is very popular and is taken very seriously by the students!
- ☐ Special Helper: For all other little jobs you may need a helper. This is always the favorite in my classroom as there are all sorts of little opportunities that pop up for students to help out with, and they just love being the 'special person' who gets to do them! A note of warning: be sure to keep track of who has already been the special helper due to its popularity, or rotate jobs in a systematic way!

CHAPTER 3: FUN GETTING-TO-KNOW-YOU ACTIVITIES!

Now this is where the real fun begins! We have talked about all of the rules, routines, and preparation, and now here is a feast of activities to help make your first day and weeks of teaching a real success! The first week of school is a wonderful time to really get to know your students before the demands of a heavy curriculum set in, so sit back, plan, and enjoy your students!

Please note: I have attempted to indicate the grade level that would be appropriate for each activity. However, many of the activities can be modified for different age levels. Any activities with accompanying reproducibles are included in the Appendix at the back of this handbook and are indicated by ★ beside their title.

Jar of Jelly Beans (Gr. 1-3)

Have a large jar of jelly beans/marbles/candies/blocks/lego at the front table. When the students enter the room, they get to make a guess as to how many jelly beans are in the jar on a piece of paper. Record the children's guesses on the board beside their names. This can be an easy way to introduce students to graphing. The children can make a bar graph indicating their guesses as compared to that of the other students, and later find out who was closest to the actual amount! The child who has the closest guess gets to help you to distribute the jelly beans/candies or other treat equally to the rest of the class for everyone to share!

Mystery Gift (Gr. 1-3)

Bake a plate of cookies or some other treat for your new class and then wrap it in a large box with a big ribbon. Put the box at the front of the room where everyone can see it, and begin a discussion about "I wonder what's in the box?!" Once everyone has had at least one guess (and the discussion can become quite hilarious – I've had guesses about baby elephants and Dalmatians), choose 2 or 3 of the 'best listeners' help you to unwrap the gift and share with the class!

Class Collage (Gr. 1-3)

This is a fun, interactive way to get students working together and sharing information about themselves. Divide children up into groups of 4 or 5. Have each child select a piece of construction paper in their favorite colour, and put their name in black felt in the centre of the page. Give each group some magazines and ask them to find pictures of things that they love or love to do. Then put all of the finished collages together on the bulletin board to make a large classroom collage.

Secret Pals/Random Acts of Kindness (Gr. 1-6)

This is a great activity to do during the first week of school. First, brainstorm with the children different compliments we can give to each other and talk about a variety of kind and respectful words we could use to describe ourselves (descriptive adjectives). Then, read stories to the students about friendship (books by Kevin Henkes are wonderful for this!). Make a list of random acts of kindness that they could do for each other (that cost little or no money). Then, have the children label a large envelope clearly with their name and decorate it with at least 3 descriptive adjectives to describe themselves. Put all of their envelopes along the bottom of one of your bulletin boards. Then, have each child write his/her name on a small piece of paper to be put into a hat. Each child draws out a name; this will be their secret pal for the week. The students can write secret little compliments to their pals each morning as their warm-up when they first enter the room and last thing before they go home at the end of the day. My students absolutely love this activity! The secret pals reveal themselves at the end of the week. Note: Be sure to monitor this activity carefully until it becomes a routine, so that a child is not left out when a secret pal does not participate. Alternatively, for children in older grades, I give each child a first-name checklist of their classmates and challenge them to write one genuine compliment for each member of the class within the first two weeks of school. This is a wonderful way to help students become more aware of noticing positive qualities in each other, therefore contributing to a warm and accepting classroom climate.

Ball Toss (Gr. 1-4)

This is a fun, interactive way to begin the year! Use a soft ball such as a nerf ball and have the students sit in a large circle on the floor. Begin by tossing the ball to someone across from you while introducing yourself and saying your favorite food, sport, color, animal, etc. That person then tosses the ball to someone else, introduces him or herself, and says their favorite thing. Continue until everyone has introduced themselves. As a fun follow-up, see if the students can remember their neighbor favorite food, sport, etc. for that round. Shuffle spots and then play again!

The Name Game (Gr. 1-6)

The objective of this activity is for the students to learn each other's names. Have the students sit in a circle so they can easily see each other's faces. One person says his/her name. Then the person next to him/her says their name in addition to the first person's name. The third person says their name in addition to the first two names, etc. It's a very simple activity but a quick and effective method of learning everyone's names right from the start!

Memory Name Game (Gr. 2-4)

This is a fun way for students to get to know each other. Have each student write his/her name on two index cards. Divide students into small groups. Instruct each group to combine and shuffle their name cards before putting them face down on the floor in front of them. The students take turns turning two cards up at a time. If the two names match, they get to keep those cards. If they don't, they have to turn them over and try again next time. At the end, the player with the most cards wins. When they are finished, have the children return to their seats (with their original own 2 name cards) and form new groups.

Secret Student (Gr. 2-6) ★

To begin this activity, have the students fill in the Secret Student form (this may need to be modified depending on your grade level). Collect all of the forms (be sure the students have put their names on them!) and then redistribute randomly. Have each child read out one form and see if anyone can guess who the Secret Student is! Students can keep track each time they guess correctly at their desks on a small piece of paper. The children who get at least 5 secret students correctly earn a small prize or privilege! (Appendix, page a.21)

Partner Puzzle (Gr. 2-6)

Have each student find a partner, and tell partners to stand back-to-back just far enough away not to be touching each other. Let students know that they will not be touching each other for this entire game. Then, call out directions which request students to find different positions in relation to their partner, such as "elbow to elbow" or "foot to foot". Make your directions progressively more difficult to follow as time goes on by calling out requests for "ear to ankle". Students can change partners after several directions, learn their new partner's name, and continue the activity several times with different classmates.

T-Shirt Activity (Gr. 2-6)

The students design a 't-shirt' made of construction paper. Then, they fill in various types of information about themselves. This may include information on the left sleeve about the kinds of foods they like to eat, their favorite holiday around the collar of the shirt, and so on. This can be decided by you in advance or student-generated. Students should fill in all of this information but not their name. The teacher puts all of these t-shirts on display on a 'clothesline' across the room, and the students must go around and guess which t-shirt belongs to whom. The students that guess them all correctly win a prize or a privilege. Then, students can introduce themselves and tell one piece of information from their t-shirt. (You can place a sticker beside this piece of information on their shirt after they have spoken as this will help you in the next activity!) Instruct the other students to listen carefully, as the next activity will depend on their remembering this information!

Summer Journal Writing (Gr. 2-6)

Another fun way to get to know your students while gaining some insight into their writing abilities right from the start is to begin journal writing the first week. Have students decorate their journals in any way they wish (within reason, of course) to help students gain a sense of ownership over their writing. Then provide journal prompts (if students seem to need these) that will help you to learn more about them, such as:

"The best thing I did during the summer was . . ."

"What I enjoyed most about school last year was . . ."

"This year I hope . . ."

Interviews (Gr. 2-6)

This activity can be modified for the different grade levels. Simply pair children up, have them ask one another predetermined questions (either class generated or teacher-generated), and then introduce their partner to the class with the information they've learned.

Mystery Door (Gr. 3-6) ★

Seal about 30 questions in 30 separate envelopes, asking information about the school, the teachers, the students' summer vacations, their favorite sport, etc. Then post these randomly outside your classroom door. As students enter the classroom, invite them to choose one envelope to open at their desk. They then have 5 to 10 minutes to work out the answer by collaborating quietly with their neighbors and then share their answers with the class. (Appendix, pages a.14-a.18)

Find Someone Who . . . (Gr. 3-6) ★

These activities are very easy to make up, and are excellent for helping students to get to know one another better. The objective is for students to fill in the answers to all of the criteria on their sheets: for example, "Find someone who loves black licorice." The nice thing about these activities is that they can be easily adapted to special themes and used throughout the year as well. (Appendix, pages a.19-a.20)

Classroom Quilt (Gr. 3-6)

This is a wonderful way to decorate your bulletin board with information about your new students! Put a large piece of paper up on your wall and distribute one piece of square paper to each student (these could be white or have your students choose their favorite colour). Inside the 4 edges of the paper, the students write 4 sentences about themselves – you can brainstorm as a class to decide what information they would like to include. In the middle of the square the students write their name in their favorite colour and using any lettering they wish (bubble, script, block), and then illustrate their four sentences around their name. Put the squares up on the paper to form a patchwork quilt! (A variation could be to have the students glue yarn around their square first or actually stitch their squares to the butcher paper).

Classroom Scavenger Hunt (Gr. 2-3)

Give the students a chance to explore their new classroom with this activity. Put the children in pairs and have them answer a list of questions about your classroom by walking around, looking at, and touching things in the room. Then, talk about what they found as a large group and clarify any questions the students might have about where things are in the classroom.

Partner Switch (Gr. 3-6)

This activity works best if the students are sitting on chairs in a circle so that they can see each other. One student is 'it' and stands in the middle of the circle. (S)he calls out one thing that students might have in common, such as "Anyone who is wearing yellow, switch seats." The person who is 'it' must find a seat before the others, or (s)he is 'it' again for the next round. It may be helpful to either brainstorm a list of things as a class that they might have in common before beginning the game to give students more options and ideas. Alternatively, the "Find Someone Who" or "Human Bingo" activity pages in the Appendix may give you some ideas.

Two Facts and a Fib (Gr. 3-6)

This is a really fun activity to do just after summer holidays but is best suited to upper elementary classes. The students write down two things that they actually did or things that really happened to them during their summer holidays this year and one thing that they would like to have done but didn't. Each child reads out his/her three 'facts' and the rest of the class needs to figure out which of the three is the fib. Alternatively, the students can walk around the classroom telling their facts and fibs to other classmates to find out how many people can guess which fact was not true!

Guess That Person Bingo (Gr. 3-6) ★

As a follow-up to the t-shirt activity, it's fun to test the students' knowledge of their classmates by playing a game of bingo. List all of the students' names on the chalkboard (the students will enjoy seeing if they can stump you on THEIR names!), and give students a blank bingo card. Have them fill in the squares with one student's name for each space (no doubles allowed). Then, call out one piece of information about one of their classmates. If they know who the information is about and have his/her name on their card, they get to put a marker on it. Continue until someone gets bingo. To win the game, the student needs to tell the names of the students (s)he has marked on their card. Have students switch seats and play another round! (Appendix, page a.23)

Something in Common (Gr. 4-6) ★

For this activity, the students must walk around and find something they have in common with each member of the class and write it down. The first person to find 10 different people with whom they have something in common wins! (Appendix, page a.24)

A "Cheezy" Memory Book (Gr. 1-6) ★

One of my students' first homework assignments of the year is to order pizza with their families and then bring an empty medium-sized pizza box to school. We then label the pizza box clearly with the child's name, and this becomes their Memory Box for the year. (Be sure to line the bottom of the pizza box with wax paper.) Then, throughout the year whenever a child completes a project or assignment which (s)he is particularly proud of, we add it to the pizza box face-down. I also add a lot of the getting-to-know-you activities we do at the beginning of the year, 'special occasions' pages throughout the year (samples are included in the Appendix for you), and an autograph page at the end. Then, at the end of the year I add a front page photo of the child from their first day in my classroom, a final note from me and coil bind all of the pages together. The children then have a wonderful keepsake from their year! (Appendix, pages a.41-a.45)

Human Bingo (Gr. 3-6) ★

Give each student a copy of the "Human Bingo" card. Then the students walk around and try to find other people who, for example, wake up at 7:00 a.m. Each time they find a person who answers yes to their question, they get to put their name in that box (as a marker). The first person to fill in their card completely and correctly needs to tell the rest of the class what they learned about their classmates. (Appendix, page a.25)

Biopoems (Grades 4-6) ★

Making a biographical poem is a wonderful way to get acquainted with your students. But be sure to make time for it. With a poem of eleven lines, you can expect to take up to a two-hour period to get them finished. The poem is strictly about students themselves, so it is useful to do some preliminary work on adjectives and expressing feelings. You will need sheets of colored construction paper, scissors, glue, colored markers, and (if desired), glitter pens and other decorations. Introduce and model the biopoem and then brainstorm adjectives to describe people together. Instruct the students to make a rough copy for you to look at first, and then make a good copy which they will cut out and paste onto their construction paper. While the students are working, go around and take pictures of the students to put above their poems on the construction paper. The students can then decorate their poems. Again, as a follow-up activity, these poems can be collected at the end of class and then randomly handed out the next class. The students need to read each poem (omitting the first line and the last two) and the other students must try to guess whose poem it is! These poems are a great way to brighten your classroom and feature your new students. (Appendix, pages a.26-a.27)

Time Capsules (All Grades) ★

I love to do this activity at the beginning of the year, and then give the capsules back to the students at the end of their year to demonstrate the growth they have experienced. To do this activity, I ask each student to bring an empty paper towel role to school, along with five small items that can fit inside which represent 'who they are'. In class, we brainstorm ideas of items that students could bring in to get them started, such as family pictures or magazine photos of favorite foods, activities, sports, hobbies, or games. Small figurines, a medal the child won, or a badge (s)he earned at Brownies or Boy Scouts also make great additions to the time capsule. Encourage your students to be creative. Also, set this up as a home/school project to help parents get involved from the beginning of the year. I have included both a letter home to parents and a sample activity students can do to put into their time capsules in the Appendix for you to adapt for your own class and grade level. (Appendix, pages a.28-a.29)

Mandalas (Grades 3-6) ★

I have found this activity to be a wonderful way to gain insight about my students at the beginning of the year, and they make a wonderful display for Open House or Parent-Teacher Interviews. In various spiritual traditions, a mandala is a teaching tool, often made of sand. For our purposes, a mandala is a visual representation of who students are as a person. Usually circular in format, a mandala is a balanced collage of student-designed pictures which illustrate who they are, often accompanied by a written explanation in the form of an "I Am Poem." I have included a sample of one of these poems in addition to several templates for this project from which you can and your students can choose. Here is how I approach teaching mandalas to my students:

1. As always, I show exemplary examples of the project before we begin
2. My students and I brainstorm numerous ideas for each section of the "Mandala Poetry" activity page, which they then complete independently with vocabulary that they feel suits their own individual personality. You can use topics such as "If you were an: animal, gem, plant, country, food, car/vehicle, or type of weather" for these poems. The possibilities depend on which concepts you feel your students manage effectively.
3. Finally, students are able to visually represent each line of their poem in the circular template (or another version students may design themselves in the upper elementary grades), filling each space with colour. It is also necessary to take some time at this point to discuss with students how different colors make them feel and which colors they feel represent their own unique personality.
4. I then mount the finished circular mandalas on large sheets of construction paper with the students' poetry below. I guarantee you will be pleased – and enlightened – by the results!

★ This project usually takes approximately five thirty-minute periods to complete, including time for revisions to student poetry and mandala design. At the beginning of the school year, I have found that spending thirty minutes each morning on this motivating activity to be a wonderful way to begin the day!

(Appendix, pages a.30-a.34)

Personal Presentations (Grades 1-3) ★

The introduction of Personal Presentations is a wonderful way to begin the year! The goal of a Personal Presentation is to celebrate the life of one of the children in your class on a specific day each week (or, depending how many children are in your class, every second week) throughout the year, and in many ways is like a special 'show and tell' for students. They love it!

For the students' presentations, I recommend parents use a large piece of poster board and help their child to paste pictures of family, favorites, collections, and/or significant events and/or successes their child has achieved outside of school. (I will provide poster paper for parents upon request.) During the presentation, the student simply explains what the pictures are of on their poster before showing and talking about any other meaningful items they have brought to show their classmates. Nerves usually dissipate quickly when talking about favorite things and the class is really interested in learning about their classmates, so management is usually not an issue! Students can then take this poster back home with them immediately following their presentation.

In my classroom, the presentations usually take place after the morning recess on Fridays, from approximately 11:15 – 11:25 a.m. Following the student's mini presentation, the students in our class write three sentences about what we learned about our classmate that day. I have the students keep a notebook especially for Personal Presentations. This way, at the end of the year each child has a wonderful keepsake of all of their classmates! Finally, we then enjoy a light snack provided by the special student. We are usually finished shortly before dismissal at 11:45 a.m. This is a wonderful way to end the school week!

To help facilitate easy organization, on "Meet the Teacher Night", I post a sign-up sheet on my blackboard for parents to select a day that would be suitable for them on one Friday during the year. I have included a sample sign-up sheet, along with an explanation letter to parents for you in the Appendix. It is also the responsibility of the student presenting to provide a snack of his/her choice for the class to be enjoyed following their presentation. This is often a way for the student to share his or her favorite snack with the rest of the children in your class!

I will often do my own Personal Presentation at the end of the first week of school for two reasons: first, to model how they are done, and secondly, to help my students learn more about their teacher. Be careful not to schedule Personal Presentations on the same days as other school events, or during the same week as special dates such as Halloween or Valentine's Day, as the intention is to make this the highlight of the class's week in celebration of this student. (It is also overwhelming for both you and your students to have too many special events in one school week!) I also send home a reminder for the parents at least one week before their child's special day. Templates for all the letters to the parents required for this activity are in the Appendix on pages a.36 to a.38.

Surprise Class Cooking Project (Grades 1-6) ★

The idea of bringing food into the classroom is not only motivating to your students, but it is also a wonderful way to build a sense of community and strengthen reading and writing skills. Depending on what you are studying at the beginning of the year, this activity can be adjusted to suit your own curriculum and can also be used throughout the year. In the fall, for example, I will often work with the theme of apples for several weeks in language arts. This topic lends itself nicely to baking apple pies, apple cookies, or making caramel apples. I will first find a great recipe. Then I send a 'secret note' home with each child explaining to parents that I would like to surprise my students with a cooking project. On their note is one measured ingredient I would like the child to bring to school on a given day. A copy of this letter is included for you in the Appendix. What a wonderful sense of excitement and mystery there is in my classroom on the morning of that day as children arrive with small baggies of cinnamon, apples, and baking powder! On the morning that the cooking project is scheduled, each child is given a blank recipe template and we begin to list the ingredients they have brought. I have found that using the overhead works wonderfully for this, with each child completing a copy for themselves. At this point, I still have not told them what we are making, and the students are busy making predictions while reading and writing – what a wonderful way to learn! After we write each line of the procedure together, the child who has brought that ingredient is invited to come up to the table at the front of my classroom to complete that stage of the recipe. When we are finished, the students have of course figured out the name of the recipe. I am always sure to credit the class for creating the dish by adding "By Mrs. Friesen's Class" under the title of the recipe. Bake and enjoy!

★ Be careful to keep track of ingredients as they come in, and if you know there is a chance several will not come in on time ensure that you have extras on hand to avoid hurt feelings or embarrassment. Nobody needs to know that the teacher provided the child's ingredient. Alternatively, some children will be immediately willing to share their ingredient if they notice that one of their classmates is without! (Appendix, pages a.39-a.40)

CHAPTER 4: GENERAL CLASSROOM MANAGEMENT

TIPS TO ENSURE SUCCESS!

In his international analysis including 83 different studies, Veenman (1984) discovered that "the most seriously perceived problem of beginning teachers was classroom discipline" (p. 153). Research carried out by other scholars has come to the same conclusion (Dollase, 1992; Housego & Badali, 1996; Nielbrand, Horn, & Holmes, 1992). Continued difficulties with classroom management are reflected in current articles and studies focused on beginning teacher experiences (Black, 2004; Feiman-Nemser, 2003; Frieberg, 2002; Johnson & Kardos, 2002; Renard, 2003; Romano & Gibson, 2006; Sargent, 2003). Being a beginning teacher myself not too long ago, and based on discussions I have had with many other beginning teachers, I concur with the findings of this research. Wong and Wong (1998) hold that "classroom management refers to all things that a teacher does to organize students, space, time, and materials so that instruction in content and student learning can take place" (p. 84). Good management is key to a pleasant, relaxed working atmosphere for you and your students, yet it seems difficult to establish because "good classroom management is nearly invisible" (Frieberg, 2002, p. 58). In this chapter, I have attempted to make explicit and very visible as many practical tips as possible to help make your first year of managing your classroom a success.

Here are three important tips for your first year as a classroom teacher:

- ✓ Deal with any problems immediately – don't put them off! Other students will take their cue from how you handle (or choose not to handle) each situation.
- ✓ Focus on *prevention* of problems by anticipating possible difficulties rather than on punishment.
- ✓ Grow eyes in the back of your head – quickly! Keep an active eye on everything that's going on in the classroom!

Here are some more general classroom management tips:

- ✓ Organize your classroom *well* at the beginning of the year. This will save you running around like a chicken with its head cut off just prior to your lessons and then feeling frazzled with the students!
- ✓ A well-managed classroom is a predictable environment for children.
- ✓ Remain genuinely positive and friendly – yet firm.
- ✓ Laugh! Keep your sense of humour.
- ✓ Be flexible. If something isn't working, don't be afraid to change it after a healthy try. On the other hand, be careful not to make too many drastic changes too quickly, especially with regard to seating arrangement and rules. Talk to the students, ask them what they think is working well and why (classroom meetings are a great way to do this).
- ✓ Give directions clearly and simply. As a general rule, give only *two* directions at a time.
- ✓ Be prepared and well-organized in lessons.
- ✓ Keep children busy in a relaxed and pleasant atmosphere.
- ✓ Establish and maintain rules, routines, and expectations as outlined in Chapter 2.

The Characteristics of a Well-Managed Classroom

1. Students are deeply involved with their work, especially with academic, teacher-led instruction.
2. Students know what is expected of them and are generally successful.
3. There is relatively little wasted time, confusion, or disruption.
4. The climate of the classroom is work-oriented, but relaxed and pleasant.

"Remember that children are basically good, and that inappropriate behavior is a purposeful response to a need for attention, power, revenge or avoidance of failure"

(ATA Handbook, p. 13).

Time Management

How well you manage your time is key to running a smooth classroom, but it is also important in successfully maintaining a healthy balance with your personal life. Expect to put in long hours as a beginning teacher – it's a steep learning curve and the only way you will learn what works for you is by 'doing the time'! However, you are going to find that it becomes difficult to give your personal life the attention it needs, too. Be sure to schedule in your own personal time as carefully as you would any of the subjects you teach, or you could quickly suffer from burn-out.

Here are some healthy tips for effective time management:

- ✓ Learn to say "NO!" during your first year, especially with regard to too much extra-curricular involvement.
- ✓ Break down large tasks into small ones and do a little each day.
- ✓ Plan your lessons at the same time and at the same place every week (at home or at school).
- ✓ Do not be afraid to ask a lot of questions about how other teachers plan and manage their time. One beginning teacher stated how she didn't want to "look as if we don't know what we're doing, even if we don't. As a result, we shy away from advice, and we don't actively seek the help and support of those who know the tricks of the trade" (Mazur, 2007, p. 14). Remember, you are not alone, and you shouldn't be afraid to admit that you are new to this profession.
- ✓ Become a list person and make one for yourself at the end of each day so that you have clear goals in mind when you are fresh the next morning.
- ✓ Have a clear routine for transitions between classes. What is expected of students when transitioning from science to language arts? From one classroom to another? Have you modeled and practiced clear expectations for your students so that they can be successful?
- ✓ Think of a variety of quick and easy ways to get student's attention when you need to speak or are ready to begin a lesson – be creative here! Here are a list of some possibilities that may work for you:
  - ☆ Count down from 10 to "zero noise" – everyone needs to have their hand up in the air and eyes on you before you reach zero.
  - ☆ Say, "Freeze please!"

- ☆ Teach students to stop, look, and listen.
- ☆ Ring a bell.
- ☆ Clap a pattern (students repeat after you).
- ☆ Play music.
- ☆ Say, "Put your finger on your nose/hands on your head if you can hear me!"
- ☆ Honk a bicycle horn (if your classroom walls are thick!).
- ☆ Use noise makers.
- ☆ Use a hook such as "You know, I have a question that I've been thinking about . . ."
- ☆ Begin singing a Christmas song . . . in June.
- ☆ And my personal favorite. Say, "Smile if you can hear me!" In response I get a sea of beautiful little smiling faces beaming back at me!
- ☆ And finally, when in a panic for time, ask yourself, "Would anything really terrible happen if I didn't do this?" If the answer is no, don't do it (Metropolitan Nashville Education Association, 1987).
- ☆ Your own ideas: ______________________________

PLANNING

You will need to do two different types of planning, short term (weekly/monthly) and long term (yearly). Be sure to ask your principal what his/her requirements and suggestions are before you begin:

- ☐ Do lesson plans need to be turned in to the principal?
- ☐ Do yearly plans need to be?
- ☐ Is there any preference regarding what type of plan book you will be using?

How effectively you plan will determine how effective your teaching will be. Take the time to develop well-thought-out lessons. Write them out step by step in the beginning so that the development of your lesson is clear in your mind and makes sense to the students. Sample lesson plan, day plan, weekly plan and year plan templates are included in the Appendix for your use on pages a.50 to a.56.

> The margin for misbehaviour in your classroom is greatly reduced when kids are on task, challenged, understand your directions and feel there is purpose to their work.

Here are some planning tips to help you to manage your classroom:

- ✓ Create a pattern for a smooth start each day. This could be in the form of:
  - ☆ Calendar time (for younger children) when you discuss the temperature outside, the day of the week, how many days of school we've had, and/or learn a poem/sing a song chorally.
  - ☆ A list of 3 directions listed on the board. This could include sharpening pencils, getting book(s) ready, and reading silently.
  - ☆ Have students write in a journal to you, which you can then reply to once a week or more.
  - ☆ A morning meeting where you discuss the schedule for the day and/or any upcoming events.
- ✓ Be sure to work from curriculum guides and approved teacher guides specifically designed for your grade level.
- ✓ Plan one subject at a time, and plan for the entire week or for the next two weeks. I still only plan for one week at a time because things seem to change so much during the week, or I think of new ideas!
- ✓ Keep only *one* calendar for all personal and professional commitments!
- ✓ Plan in pencil.
- ✓ Decide how you will organize your lessons. Your school may have a required plan book. If not, you can either buy a commercially prepared plan book at teacher supply stores, or make one of your own. I made my own with subject headings already written in each section, which cuts down on planning time. For an example, please see the Appendix.
- ✓ Ask other teachers at your grade level how they plan.
- ✓ Allow for a variety of different learning experiences for your students by using a variety of teaching strategies. In Frieberg's 2002 article, he notes that "new teachers are most familiar with teacher-centred instructional strategies and often revert to them when under pressure. The good news is that, with time and experience, teachers can learn to use more student-centred instructional approaches" (p. 58). The following list may spark your enthusiasm and creativity when planning:

Teaching Strategies

Debate	Cooperative learning	Pets
Autobiography	Invention	Films and videos
CD's/tapes	Brainstorming	Student ideas
Quiz	Competition	Letter to expert
Graphs	Drama	Correspondence
Advertisements	Albums	Puppets
Plays	Overhead transparencies	Dialogue
Case study	Meditation	Interviewing
Skits	Puzzles	Computers
Jigsaw	Sand table	Bingo
Posters	Brochures	Murals
Choral reading	Book review	Pantomime
Team teaching	Manipulatives	Cartooning
Mind mapping	Independent projects	Journal writing
Reports	Centres	Games
Crafts	Replica	Simulation

Have activities on hand at all times for students to do if they are finished their work early. In my classroom, I have a "Mind Candy" centre where I place enrichment math, language, and art activities in manila folders. Here are some ideas to get you started:

- ☆ Draw or list as many objects/animals/things in this room/at a circus as you can that start with the letter "B".
- ☆ List all the things in your bedroom/bathroom/living room/backyard.
- ☆ Write as many adjectives as you can think of.
- ☆ List one proper noun for every letter of the alphabet.
- ☆ Write a riddle (provide a funny example).
- ☆ List or draw as many cartoon characters as you can.
- ☆ List all of the provinces and territories in Canada.
- ☆ Draw and label as many different dogs as you can.
- ☆ Complete unfinished assignments.

☆ Read stories and poems.
☆ Go to the listening centre.
☆ Crossword puzzles.
☆ Play educational games.
☆ Word searches.
☆ Brain stretchers.
☆ Experiment with math manipulatives.
☆ Write a story.
☆ Make a card for someone they love.
☆ Fun art activities.
☆ Puzzles and riddles.

Planning for Substitute Teachers

Planning for a substitute teacher, especially when the substitute does not know your school or classroom culture well, can be a great challenge. A wonderful solution to this challenge is to have what I call a "Substitute Teacher Folder" in my classroom for substitutes to refer to when they come into my room. I have included a copy of the one I use in my own classroom in the Appendix on pages a.46 to a.49. The folder should include information such as:

- ☐ How to take attendance at your school.
- ☐ Where to find the name tags and the routine for distribution.
- ☐ What the morning routine is in your classroom.
- ☐ What the after recess routine is in your classroom.
- ☐ What the after lunch routine is in your classroom.
- ☐ What the end of the day duties are in your classroom (and where to find information about which students are your classroom helpers for these jobs at this time).
- ☐ Behavior or incentive programs established in your room and how they are run.
- ☐ What the discipline guidelines (class rules) are in your classroom.
- ☐ Names of classroom assistants, their schedules, and which children they work with.

- ☐ Names of parent helpers who come into your classroom on a regular basis and their schedule.
- ☐ What the procedures are for the hallway and for special classes including library routines, computer room procedures, and gym safety routines.
- ☐ Fire drill and lockdown procedures.
- ☐ Children with allergies, special needs, or medical concerns.
- ☐ Routines for students who finish work early.

You should also include:

- ☐ A first name checklist of the students in your classroom.
- ☐ An up-to-date class seating plan and class timetable.
- ☐ A list of the names of the other teachers and staff at your school should the substitute require any assistance.

I also include my home phone number should they have any questions or concerns, but this is entirely up to you! Just think about how easily you can make up sub plans if you have this information booklet already made!

Consequences

> "Discipline problems are minimized when students are regularly engaged in meaningful activities geared to their interests and aptitudes"
>
> (Brophy & Good, 1996)

Regardless of how clearly you teach the rules of your classroom or how many times you review them and practice them with your students, there will still be moments when students will test the boundaries if for no other reason than to see if you will follow through with the consequences you have laid out. However, there are some important points to remember about consequences:

- ☆ **Consequences are not punishment. They are a natural, fair outcome that suit the Behavior.** For example, if a student is running in the hall and there exists a very clear rule that states that no running in the halls is allowed, the consequence should be that the student go back and walk. If a student is speaking out of turn, the Behavior could first be ignored (because any attention is 'good attention' in the student's eyes). If the Behavior continues, have a short talk with the student about it. If an understanding is not reached, the student could be politely asked to wait outside of the group (i.e. at the back of the room) for the remainder of the discussion.

☆ **Consequences are extended only to the individual who has broken the rule.** If only one or two children were yelling in the hall when coming back from gym class, the entire class should not have to deal with the consequences for that action.

☆ **The consequences extended should be fair.** However, fair does not mean that the same consequences exist for all students at all times. Rather, it means that you are being **consistent**. Individual personalities and situational contexts need to be kept in mind. For example, if a student is late to class and has been late for five times in a row, the consequences for that student may be different than for the child who has never been late until today.

☆ **Avoid consequences that are related to an academic grade.** Again, consequences should relate to the Behavior in question.

☆ **Student discipline means consequences for breaking a related rule.** If a child breaks his/her pencil on the desk, the related consequence could be to write a letter of apology to his/her parents with the broken pencil inside, and a second letter to you for disrupting your class to be kept in his/her individual file.

☆ **Remember that consequences are a result of a choice the student made.** Remind students that they are in control of their situation.

☆ **Finally, it is necessary to have a series of consequences, depending on the rule broken and the seriousness of the Behavior.** Here are some examples of strategies you may use when children break the rules:

- ☐ Pause and look at the student with a "I'm watching you" stare.
- ☐ Work the student's name into whatever you are saying. For example, "Therefore, a spider is not really an insect, Tanner, because it has 8 legs."
- ☐ Physically walk over and stand by the student without interrupting what you are talking about.
- ☐ Lay a hand on the student's shoulder.
- ☐ Do NOT stop the lesson to deliver the consequence! This simply gives the student the attention (s)he was looking for.

If the Behavior continues, you may wish to:

- ☐ Hold an individual conference with the student.
- ☐ Have the student take a 'time out'.
- ☐ Remove the student from the group.
- ☐ Withhold special privileges.
- ☐ Phone parents.
- ☐ Detention (ask about your school policy on keeping students after school hours first).
- ☐ Ask the previous teacher and other teachers at your grade level for advice on the situation.
- ☐ Assignment to write five ways to correct the problem.
- ☐ If the child seems depressed or seems to be experiencing other emotional and/or social difficulties, you may wish to obtain parental permission for a referral to your school Counselor.
- ☐ Ask for administrative assistance.

> Effective teachers MANAGE their classrooms.
> Ineffective teachers DISIPLINE their classrooms.
> (Wong, H.K. & Wong, R.T., 1998, p. 83)

Classroom Management Programs

Many teachers I know have implemented management 'programs' as an added incentive for students to follow class rules. Here are two examples of such programs and how they are run:

Ten Tickets

This program has been a success in my own classroom – the students LOVE it! At the beginning of the year, I give ten tickets to each student. These are simply pieces of manila tag in a light colour, cut into strips 3cm x 12 cm. The students put their names on their tickets in a dark colored marker, and the tickets are laminated for durability. They are then kept in a special envelope inside their desk. If a rule is broken by the student, I ask him or her to give me a ticket. (To ensure class time is not taken up with this process, I simply walk over to where the disruption has occurred and lightly tap on the student's desk – he or she simply hands me a ticket and we move on). This continues for the entire week. I like this process, because the children start the week in a positive way, with 100%!

I also emphasize that it is entirely their choice if they are to keep all ten tickets, and I teach students how to be successful in this program by reviewing our five class rules. At the end of the week, I roll a 'magic die'. If a student has that number of tickets or higher, he or she earns a special privilege or reward from me. All tickets are then re-distributed (I have a job on my helper board for a student to be in charge of this), and we start fresh again the following week.

Mystery Motivator

This idea has been borrowed from one of my mentor teachers, Marjorie Andrews. Although now retired, she continues to be adored and respected by her students and peers. To run this program, you will need a blank 'one hundred grid' pasted to the outside of an envelope for each child. Inside each envelope, place a small reward such as a special bookmark, a certificate, or a treat. (It is important to keep track of what you have given to each child so that (s)he is not receiving the same reward every time). With an invisible marker, print an X on five random squares on the one hundred grid. Each time a child is 'caught doing something right' (s)he is invited to colour in one random square on the grid. This continues until (s)he has colored in all five squares with the 'invisible X's'. (S)he is then invited to open the envelope to receive the secret prize hidden inside!

Although these programs can be fun and motivating for the students, it is important to keep in mind the pros and cons of incentive programs such as these in your classroom. They can be time-consuming and expensive, and the consequence (i.e. losing a ticket) may not always match the nature or the seriousness of the Behavior. Therefore, it is important not to rely entirely on a program such as this. On the other hand, students who feel they are finally in an environment that they can control with tangible reinforcements are able to modify their Behavior with this program.

Rewarding Positive Behavior

Positive Behavior can be rewarded in a variety of ways so that there exists a careful blend of both positive and negative reinforcement in your classroom. Positive reinforcement can be rewarded either to individuals or to the entire class, depending on the situation. On the next page are some ideas to positively encourage students, and they don't cost a lot of money! Please see the Appendix, on pages a.57 to a.60, for samples of many of these rewards including "Special Person Awards" and a variety of individual student certificates for you to use or modify to suit your own teaching context and style. Enjoy!

INDIVIDUAL REWARDS	CLASS REWARDS
• A smile • Stickers • Pencils • Erasers • Penny candy • Certificate • Note to parents • Phone call home (with student listening!) • Verbal praise • A pat, handshake, or highfive • Chew gum in class for a day • Display individual work • Extra computer time • 'Special Person Award!' • Draw on chalk board • Wear 'Special Student' ribbon • Recognition from principal on morning announcements Privileges: • lunch with the teacher • extra recess • choice of where to sit • keep stuffed animal on desk • write with gel pen for a day	• Extra recess/gym/art time • Play a game the class loves • Verbal praise • Free time • Free reading time • A story from the teacher • Video • A special surprise guest • Chew gum in class for a day • Bring stuffed animals from home for a day • A class cooking project • Choose the order of subjects for a day • A walk to the park • A visit from the principal Special Class Goal: • Add marbles or scoops of popcorn to a jar – when it's full the class earns a larger reward such as a popcorn or ice-cream party • Students earn 'letters' printed on the blackboard towards spelling a particular reward, such as "ONE HALF HOUR OF FREE TIME."

A Special Class Reward:

It was an August afternoon when I came up with this idea for using a treasure chest and a treasure map in my classroom to motivate and inspire students through stories. Because I have traveled a lot and because I am a passionate storyteller, one of my students' favorite rewards is to hear about stories from my travels around the world. It dawned on me that I could use these stories not only as a way to bond with my students through sharing our stories, but also as a way to teach geography and to motivate the class. I designed a 'treasure map' and, using gold glitter glue, I created a path around the world with gold coins pasted on it at particular locations (and about 10 steps apart on the map). The trail begins in Lethbridge (where our classroom is) and ends on Crete, Greece – the location of Barbarosa's Cave where he hid his pirate treasure.

Next, I found a 'treasure chest' at a garage sale and filled it with gold cloth and stories of my travels written on scrolls tied with gold ribbon. My class had their very own magnet 'ship' and they earned spaces on the treasure map for following class rules. When we reached a gold coin, we would gather around the treasure chest. I'd pull a name out of a hat (so that everyone will have a turn by the year's end) and that child got to choose the scroll for that stop on our adventure. As we gathered around and shared the story, it became the catalyst for stories the students didn't even realize they had but which suddenly needed to be told – to each other, in their writing, in their whispers during free time. As we traveled around the world through our imaginations, we not only learned about each other and the importance of our stories in our developing classroom community, but we also learned to work together to achieve a common goal. When we reached our final destination at Barbarosa's Cave, our class earns a "Pirate Pyjama Popcorn Party." On this day, the students were invited to come dressed either as a pirate or in their pyjamas (or both!), and we would enjoy popcorn and a short movie to celebrate our accomplishments. Then our ship would return to its original 'harbour' and we'd begin our journey anew (approximately once every three months).

As a beginning teacher, I encourage you to find your own 'treasure map' in the experience that has been your life and incorporate this into your classroom in a way that will not only help your students to get to know you as a person, but which will also help you to define your own teaching style. Perhaps travel isn't your passion – maybe it's a hockey team or science. Whatever it is, I encourage you to find that something special that will make your classroom a reflection of who you are becoming as a teacher.

CHAPTER 5: STUDENT MOTIVATION

INTRINSIC OR EXTRINSIC MOTIVATION?

How you attempt to motivate your students depends on what you believe about human nature. Motivation can be either *intrinsic* or *extrinsic* in nature. Intrinsic motivation has been defined as "self-initiating and unrelated to the need for social approval or economic reward" (Stipek, 1988), whereas extrinsic motivation takes the form of an external reward such as stickers, certificates, candies, coupons, certificates, etc. I have designed the chart below to give you further examples of what characterizes these two different types of motivation:

INTRINSIC MOTIVATORS	EXTRINSIC MOTIVATORS
• uses student curiosity as a motivator • focuses on the natural, inner desire for personal competence • involves the use of mental challenges, such as problem solving, puzzles, conflicts, and mysteries	• token systems: i.e. marbles in a jar for groups or individuals • high grades • display of student work • a special guest • inviting parents in to see high quality work or sending 'warm fuzzy' notes home • positive phone calls home

It is common to see teachers utilizing a combination of these two different types of motivation in their classes. For example, a teacher may awaken children's curiosity and inner desire to learn through interesting and challenging, well-designed lessons (intrinsic motivation), while also displaying outstanding student work and rewarding the class for its hard work with a popcorn party at the end of the semester. However, it can sometimes be very difficult for the beginning teacher to maintain intrinsic motivation in their classrooms due to outside influences. For instance, knowledge that you have to cover the curriculum and trying to simply get through all of the required material tends to discourage teachers from arousing intrinsic motivation in students. It is a common error for beginning teachers to make statements such as "I know this is boring, so let's just get through it." However, the results of intrinsic motivation are an exquisite reward offered only to teachers, and from my personal experience, I can tell you that it is worth the extra effort it may take for you to foster. Here are some techniques you can use to promote students' intrinsic interests in your class:

☆ **Build genuine relationships with your students.**
Nothing will motivate a child to learn more than the bond you build with him or her. One award winning teacher stated that "the relationship between the teacher and the students is the most important element in a successful classroom" (Stone, 2005, p. 50).

☆ **Use a variety of student groupings.**
Variety is the spice of life and nowhere is this truer than in the classroom. Include individual, paired, and small group activities in your planning. This allows shy students to begin to take more risks in close encounters with peers.

☆ **Teach critical thinking skills.**
Ask higher-level questions (and questions requiring more than a yes or no answer) and encourage students to question the world around them.

☆ **Provide choice.**
Allow students to make decisions about their learning. This could mean students choosing the colour of paper/materials for an assignment, deciding on the order of assignments or subjects for the day, study topics based on personal interest, or even where to work in the classroom.

☆ **Stimulate the students.**
We have a lot of competition as teachers in today's world with video games, movies, and television. Bring the real world into the classroom, and use relevant 'kid culture' in your teaching. This could mean using elements of a popular movie to teach a lesson or as a springboard to introduce a new topic.

☆ **Invite student participation in planning.**
Although this can be tricky because we need to ensure that the objectives for each subject are being met, making that extra effort to provide students a sense of control over their environment by encouraging participation in planning their learning is a wonderful motivator. Take the time and effort to invite students' ideas and interests when planning units.

☆ **Encourage individual self-expression.**
Regardless of whether you are teaching art or science, encouraging students to put their own personal touches on projects or assignments could help to increase motivation.

☆ **Keep lessons relevant and meaningful to students' lives.**
As teachers, we are committed to teaching a mandated curriculum. However, the methods we choose to teach objectives should be meaningful to students. For example, if you are teaching a science unit on "Boats and Buoyancy," invite students to bring in pictures of family boats (or boats they may have seen on holiday) to study and discuss and, if possible, teach buoyancy by taking the students to a swimming pool to test flotation devices.

☆ **Invite a sense of playfulness and drama into your lessons.**
How you choose to encompass this into your teaching will depend on your personality and personal teaching style. For myself, when I teach science, I wear a 'mad professor wig' and lab coat, complete with black-rimmed glasses and a foreign accent. The students just love to volunteer to be the 'victims' (my own word for volunteers) for my experiments!

☆ **Emphasize each child's strengths.**
I love to 'brag up' my students, and I never miss an opportunity to tell a student how proud I am of them when they reach a challenging goal. I will never forget one of my high school English teachers telling the entire class what a great descriptive writer I was. This greatly influenced my own belief that I could write. I believe it is our responsibility as teachers to help each child to discover his/her own unique gift, and share it with the world (or at least his/her parents!)

☆ **Bring the real world into the classroom whenever possible.**
I have the travel bug and have therefore found myself backpacking and living in some exotic locations around the globe. When I teach a unit on Japan, Hong Kong, Australia, or another country with which I am at home, I bring in real foods from that country. I bring pictures into my classroom and tell stories about my adventures there. I invite in guest speakers with wonderful accents and fascinating life histories to tell their stories, and I take my students on mini field-trips in their minds to help them to explore and discover these worlds existing parallel to their own. When I teach a unit on "Small Crawling and Flying Animals," I bring in an assortment of animals both alive and preserved for us to examine, and we create a 'worm farm' in

our classroom. We explore our own backyard for small animals who have made the playground their home, and I invite pet store owners into our classroom to teach us about caring for these animals. Bring the real world into your own classroom – it truly does inspire learning.

☆ **Provide a safe, accepting learning environment.**
Take the time and care to establish and practice with your students safe and caring rules. Students will feel safe if they understand their boundaries, and if they know that you care about their wellbeing. It is equally as important to teach students that mistakes are welcome in your classroom, so that they will not be afraid to take risks in their learning. "Make school a place the students want to be; if you make learning exciting and interesting, most will want to be there" (Stone, 2005, p. 34).

☆ **Link your own life lessons and experience with your teaching.**
While on vacation in Greece one summer, I came across a little tabby cat who had made his home just outside of our hotel. Each morning, I would bring him out a little bowl of milk. This continued for the next week while we stayed at the hotel and, on the last day, I decided I would get him something special – a can of tuna from the grocery store. As I searched the aisle for the canned fish, I came across my favorite food from Greece, right next to the can of tuna. I hadn't known it came in a can and, as a result, I was able to bring back some of this wonderful food with me to Canada. I thanked that little tabby cat for this unexpected gift – if I hadn't met him, I wouldn't have made this discovery! I use this lesson in my classes with my students to teach them that sometimes, a random act of kindness comes back to you in a simple but beautiful way. The ending to this story is really the best part. I told that tabby cat story to a class of students a few years ago and just this year a little boy came to my classroom door. He came to tell me that he had nominated me for "Teacher of the Year," and then said, "See? I'm just like the little tabby cat from Greece." Personal life experiences often help to teach the best lessons.

☆ **Finally, use your creativity and imagination in your classroom.**
I have designed and use regularly a variety of games that help to teach and/or review challenging material. The main draw to these games for me is that they are flexible and not restricted to one subject area. This allows me to use them in a variety of ways in the classroom without re-creating them each time. The students love these games and beg to play them (and they don't realize how much they are learning!) On the next page are the instructions for three of the most motivational games I've come up with.

Games that Motivate and Inspire!

Classroom Jeopardy

Based on the popular TV game show, I have modified this game for classroom use. I purchased three tambourines from the dollar store in three different colors. These are placed open-face down on a table at the front of the room, and will act as 'buzzers' for our game. Elect one person to keep score for the game. Then, divide your class into three equal teams, and give each student a number from one to seven (if you have 21 students). When I call the number one, those three players come up to the front of the room standing behind the table with the tambourines. One hand is behind their back and the other by their side. (They like this stance because it makes it look like they are on a real game show!) They are asked a question and the first person to hit their buzzer (tambourine) gets to answer. If the answer is correct, they score a point for their team. If they are not correct, the correct answer is offered by the audience (this keeps everyone involved!). To minimize movement and disruption, I have found it is best to allow a minimum of three questions per number called, and mix up the order of the numbers called so that students stay on their toes! Again, the beauty of this game is that it is very versatile – I have used it to reinforce skills and concepts in a variety of subject areas across the curriculum.

Slap!

This is a fantastic game to teach new or challenging vocabulary, to review a concept in any subject, to teach phonics or basic math facts in the younger grades, or to teach students' names at the beginning of the year!

To play this game, you will need two or three fly swatters in different colors (and I like to add a bit of sparkly ribbon tied to the fly swatter for some added magic and pizzazz), and blackboard. For ease of explanation, let's assume I am wanting to review basic addition and subtraction facts to ten. I would then print random numbers from zero to ten on the blackboard. Divide the class into two teams, with a piece of masking tape on the floor to indicate the starting line. The teacher calls out a math fact (3+6=), and the first person to 'slap' the correct answer with his or her flyswatter earns a point for their team. (We often don't even keep score – it's just too much fun to play and nobody seems to care who wins anyways). This game can become quite noisy, and so I encourage 'silent cheers' as we play. A fun modification of this game is to print the words or numbers on a blank overhead transparency and play the game either projected onto the blackboard or the screen. This saves time and allows for re-use of the game. Again – this game is fun, versatile, and oh-so motivating for the students!

The Millionaire Game

I came up with this take-off on the popular game show, "Who Wants to be a Millionaire?" one day when I wanted to review a tricky science unit with my class. Many versions of this game are available for classroom use, but I prefer my 'old fashioned' paper version of the game because it is ready to use any time with very little preparation or fuss in any subject area. I made up the following templates on a large piece of cardstock, laminated them, and then attached magnets to the back of them:

Who Wants to Be a Grade ___ Millionaire?

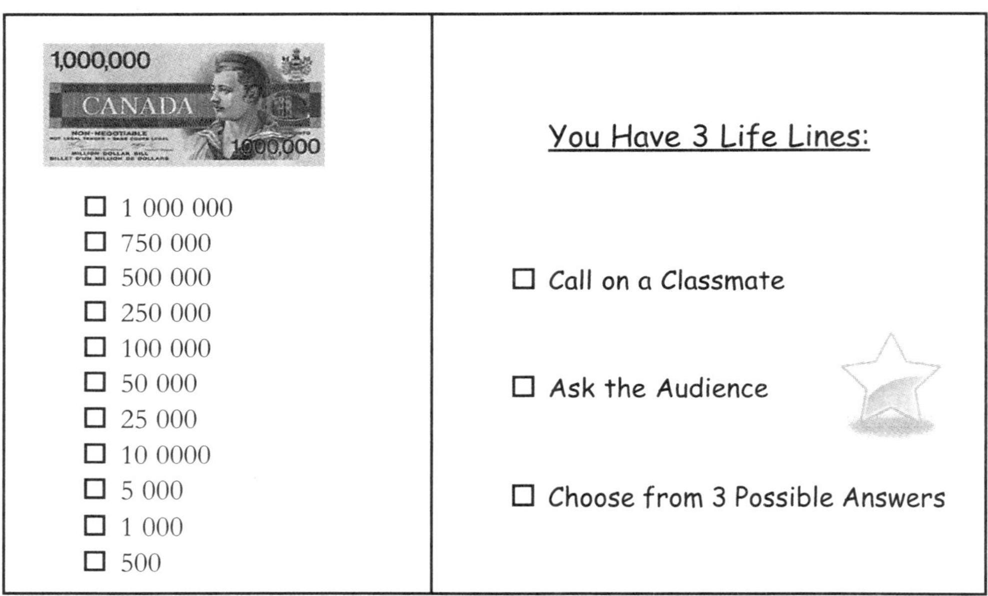

Of course, these game boards are in bright colors with stickers and other graphics to grab students' attention, along with a pretend million dollar bill on display at the top of the game which the student will win if (s)he is able to answer all questions correctly. (These novelty $1 000 000 bills are available at most dollar stores.) I then place two chairs just below where I have hung these displays, and use a magic marker as my microphone. I have all students put their name on a small piece of paper to be put in a draw. In the real game show, the audience is to answer a 'fast finger question,' so I have the students imagine they have a keyboard in front of them. They pretend they are punching in an answer as fast as they can while I draw out a student's name.

Using my very best "Regis" impersonation, I welcome my new guest to the show. The student is free to become anyone they would like to for the game show, and from wherever they wish to live. (I find that this helps to alleviate some of the stress of being in front of their classmates – I have had martians from California and astronauts from Greece on my show – those are some creative students!) I then use a student scribbler, notebook, and/or experiment write-ups (if you are reviewing science concepts) to ask questions of my guest. I begin with very simple questions to help the student gain confidence, and then move on to some of the more difficult concepts and/or vocabulary 'as the stakes get higher'. Students feel successful and supported knowing that they have the assistance of the three life lines should they get stuck.

Should (s)he answer all questions correctly, (s)he earns the (laser printed) million dollar bill. I also have a small reward for anyone who does not reach the million dollar mark. Students ask to play this game whenever they can, and so I am sure to fit it in about once every two weeks to review spelling words, phonics, science, social studies, or challenging vocabulary in all subject areas. The possibilities are endless!

Praise

One of the most effective forms of motivation comes in the form of verbal praise, if it is awarded correctly. Here are some tips on how to deliver effective praise:

- ✓ **Be honest.**
- ✓ **Be specific.** For example, rather than "Good job, Nathan" say, "Thank you for putting the chairs back at the table, Nathan. You really saved us some time by doing that without being asked!"
- ✓ **Be creative.** Not everything a child does should be described as "wonderful" or "very good". For example, instead of "Wonderful printing!" You could say, "Thank you for your extra effort in your printing, Callie. Your letters are very straight and tall, and you have a finger space between each of your words. Would you like to do some printing for a class project for me?"
- ✓ **Avoid comparing children to each other.** For example, don't say "Good for you – you are almost as fast as Riley in your math facts!"
- ✓ **Use "I" statements.** For example, "I really appreciate how quietly you walked down the hall, Ryan!"
- ✓ **Appreciate students' individual and unique efforts and abilities.** For example, "You have a special gift for solving math problems, Ashley."

Individual Needs of Students

Howard Gardner put together what he called a "theory of multiple intelligences" (1983). This term acknowledges the multifaceted profile of the human mind, and it is highly applicable to the students you will be teaching in your classroom. According to Gardner, there exist 8 intelligences:

- ✓ verbal-linguistic: word intelligence
- ✓ logical- mathematical: number and reasoning intelligence
- ✓ visual-spatial: picture intelligence
- ✓ musical-rhythmic: music and rhythm intelligence
- ✓ bodily-kinesthetic: body intelligence
- ✓ interpersonal: social intelligence
- ✓ intrapersonal: self intelligence
- ✓ naturalist: natural environment intelligence

Gardner stresses that although intelligence is a biological function, it is inseparable from the cultural context in which it exists. To be an effective classroom teacher, you will need to first observe your students informally on a day-to-day basis to gather important information about their unique intelligences . It is then your responsibility to design learning experiences which incorporate a wide variety of teaching strategies to ensure that you reach all of your students.

For examples of strategies you can use to incorporate the multiple intelligences in your classroom teaching, please see the many helpful resources listed on the following page:

> Teachers "have to acquire a variety of teaching approaches and of materials that will allow any group of students to learn in ways that they individually presently favour while making it necessary and reasonably agreeable for each of them to develop other ways of acquiring knowledge and skill, especially since all of them will need to be able to learn in varied ways throughout their lives"
>
> (MacDonald & Healy, 1999, p.161).

Resources on Multiple Intelligence

Armstrong, Thomas (1994). *Multiple Intelligences in the Classroom.* Alexandria, VA: Assoc. for Supervision and Curriculum Development.

Alberta Learning (2000). *Teaching Students Who are Gifted and Talented: Programming for Students with Special Needs.* Alberta Learning, Special Education Branch.

Campbell, L., Campell, B., & Dickerson, D. (1996). *Teaching and Learning Through Multiple Intelligences.* Needham Heights, MA: Allyn & Bacon.

Gardner, Howard. (1993). *Frames of Mind: The Theory of Multiple Intelligences.* New York: Basic Books.

Gardner, Howard. (1993) *Multiple Intelligences: The Theory in Practice.* New York: Basic Books.

Haggerty, Brian A. (1995). *Nurturing Intelligences: A Guide to Multiple Intelligences Theory and Teaching.* Menlo Park, CA: Innovative Learning, Addison-Wesley.

Lazear, David (1992). *Seven Ways of Knowing: Teaching for Multiple Intelligences.* Arlington Heights, IL: IRI/Skylight Training.

Lazear, David (1994). *Seven Pathways of Learning: Teaching Students and Parents about Multiple Intelligences.* Tucson: Zephyr Press.

Torrence, E. Paul, & Sisk, A. Dorothy (1997). *Gifted and Talented Children in the Regular Classroom.* Buffalo, NY: Creative Education Foundation Press.

Winebrenner, Susan (1992). *Teaching Gifted Kids in the Regular Classroom.* Minneapolis, MN: Free Spirit Publishing Inc.

Students experiencing difficulty

In addition to the many gifts and talents the children in your classroom will have, it may be surprising to discover the wide range of difficulties students can experience in the regular classroom setting. These difficulties could take the form of falling behind in a specific subject such as reading or math, or be more general in nature, such as difficulty sustaining concentration for age-appropriate assignments and activities. Here are some examples of difficulties students in elementary school may experience, and steps you should take when you first notice a learning or Behavior difficulty:

Examples of Difficulties

- ☆ communication skills (e.g., articulation, expression, vocabulary)
- ☆ deaf and/or hard of hearing
- ☆ vision
- ☆ English as a second language (ESL)
- ☆ fine motor skills (e.g., cutting, coloring, manipulation)
- ☆ gross motor skills (e.g., balancing, climbing, crawling)
- ☆ specific subject (e.g., math, reading, writing)
    - ☆ math – general, data, numeration, operation, etc.
    - ☆ reading – comprehension, fluency, expressiveness, etc.
    - ☆ writing – capitalization, punctuation, conventions, etc.
- ☆ memory difficulties
- ☆ impulsivity
- ☆ attention difficulties
- ☆ co-operation skills
- ☆ anger management difficulties
- ☆ lack of participation in group activities
- ☆ physical aggression
- ☆ dishonesty
- ☆ truancy

Gather Information/Assessment

When you (or a parent of a child in your class) find you have a concern about a student's academic progress or Behavior, it is important that you first gather and assess as much information about that student as possible. This is to ensure that you understand the student's learning strengths and needs, and develop an appropriate educational program. "Formal assessment requires the integration of information from several sources such as testing, observation, interviews, analysis of history and home environment, and academic records. Assessment may be viewed as a process which continues if warranted until problems are overcome and solutions are effectively implemented" (Alberta Education Standards for psycho-educational assessment, 1994, p. 3). Once you have gathered this information, it may be helpful to discuss what you have learned with your principal.

Consult with Student and Parents

Once you have a clearer picture of the specific difficulty the student is experiencing, hold a discussion with the parents and with the child. During this meeting, ask if hearing and/or vision tests are up to date, and share information collected with parents. Discuss the possibility of difficulties in the past and work together to implement a plan for this year. If you feel you have enough information at this stage, plan and implement strategies to support the student's difficulty. Here are some suggestions for instructional modifications you can make in your classroom:

Behavior Strategies

The student might . . .

- ✓ agree on and respond to a confidential teacher cue which indicates inappropriate out-of-desk wandering.
- ✓ be allowed a variety of choices within the confines of the rules.
- ✓ be coached to choose partners who are successful in interpersonal communications.
- ✓ be isolated from classmates if roaming.
- ✓ be offered different approaches to assessment.
- ✓ be rewarded for positive verbal communications with teachers and other students.
- ✓ be part of a special group who will share job responsibility.
- ✓ chart on-task work progress; teacher assisted.
- ✓ have two desks in the classroom and they can only be in one or the other.
- ✓ identify a buddy to work with to imitate appropriate planned Behavior.
- ✓ list impulsive behaviors being exhibited and write an agreement to reduce these behaviors.
- ✓ list the logical consequences of inappropriate Behavior (e.g., loss of friends, negative reputation).
- ✓ lose recess or noon-time privileges (if parent has approved) when aggression is exhibited.
- ✓ make up class time that is missed due to lates, wandering, etc.,
- ✓ set time limits for specific task completion.
- ✓ use a personal journal in which to record feelings, action plans, etc.

- ✓ utilize numerous options for anger management (e.g., ignoring, leaving the situation, count down from ten, colour with a red crayon).
- ✓ work in an isolated area, whenever necessary (e.g., a time-out area, a desk beside the teacher's desk).
- ✓ work in close proximity to the teacher.
- ✓ work on small sections of the project at a time so as not to be overwhelmed or frustrated (chunking).

(Above listed strategies reprinted from *Sirs SPED IPP Strategies,* Lethbridge School District #51)

ATTENTION-DEFICIT STRATEGIES:

- ✓ Provide seating in close proximity to teacher.
- ✓ Provide seating away from possible distractions.
- ✓ Play games requiring concentration.
- ✓ Be specific, consistent, and systematic in expectations and actions.
- ✓ Set time limits for task completion.
- ✓ Allow students to take breaks during tests and assignments.
- ✓ Have students repeat back instructions.
- ✓ Provide shorter directions.
- ✓ Break down larger tasks into smaller, more manageable chunks.
- ✓ Provide a task checklist or other visual reminder/cue.
- ✓ Use multiple testing sessions for comprehensive tests.
- ✓ Post daily schedules consistently.
- ✓ Use advance organizers.
- ✓ Provide directions in written form.
- ✓ Allow student to work in short blocks of time.

READING STRATEGIES:

- ✓ Break larger assignments into smaller chunks.
- ✓ Substitute required assignments.
- ✓ Reduce the amount of reading required.

- ✓ Use large-print editions of texts.
- ✓ Allow student to tape record lessons and/or class discussions.
- ✓ Adjust the amount of copying.
- ✓ Use a listening centre to encourage confidence.
- ✓ Repeat directions or have the student repeat directions.
- ✓ Read aloud to an adult, peer, book buddy, or stuffed animal.
- ✓ Shorten directions.
- ✓ Give addition time to complete assignments.
- ✓ Allow a reading buddy and/or peer tutor.
- ✓ Read in a distraction-free area.
- ✓ Read into an audio tape and then listen.
- ✓ Provide for opportunity to re-read.
- ✓ strategies to enhance recall (e.g., cloze activities, retell, summary).

WRITING STRATEGIES:

- ✓ Reduce the amount of written work required.
- ✓ Allow for additional time to complete assignments.
- ✓ Allow for a scribe.
- ✓ Give choice in presentation of writing format.
- ✓ Provide immediate reinforcement.
- ✓ Allow for a peer writing buddy.
- ✓ Provide a computer keyboard as an alternative to writing.
- ✓ Provide an alphabet printing model to be kept on the student's desk.
- ✓ Allow for spelling and punctuation errors.
- ✓ Chart success with acceptable letter size, spacing, and/or punctuation and capitalization.
- ✓ Dictate into a tape recorder.
- ✓ Use multi-sensory stimulation, such as a foil-wrapped cookie sheet with instant pudding powder sprinkled on top in which to practice printing.
- ✓ Use colored paper for writing assignments

Mathematics Strategies

- ✓ Break larger assignments into smaller chunks.
- ✓ Substitute required assignments.
- ✓ Reduce the amount of work required.
- ✓ Allow for a peer math buddy.
- ✓ Allow for additional time to complete assignments.
- ✓ Vary grading systems for homework and tests.
- ✓ Teach new concepts in advance and provide for additional review and/or practice of new concepts.
- ✓ Provide for opportunity for students to self-correct assignments.
- ✓ Allow the use of calculators.
- ✓ Increase the number of concrete manipulatives (e.g., blocks, cubes).

Assessment Procedures

If you have worked together with the parent, child, and your administration to determine and implement modifications within your classroom and these modifications have succeeded, then no further action may need to be taken. However, if after a predetermined amount of time the Behavior or difficulty has not improved, it may be time to refer the student to the student support team for testing. "The composition of the student support team will vary but may include the referring teacher, the school administrator, classroom teachers, special education teacher, school Counselor, parents and other significant stakeholders; e.g., speech-language pathologist. At the initial meeting of the students support team, which ideally includes parents, information is reviewed, the problem defined and problem solving begins" (*Teaching Students with Learning Disabilities, Alberta Education*, p.56). From here, a formal assessment may be required and an IPP (Individualized Program Plan) developed. For more information on developing IPPs, refer to the text *Teaching Students with Learning Disabilities*, Alberta Education, Special Education Branch.

CHAPTER 6: ASSESSMENT

SOME GENERAL TIPS TO GET YOU STARTED

Ask any teacher what they do not appreciate about their job, and they will more than likely tell you that it is having to assess and evaluate their students. This is because there is nothing more difficult than having to assign a simple letter grade to everything you know about the complex picture of a student's abilities, talents, and knowledge. Learning to develop assessment tools that will authentically evaluate what a child knows is a skill which will become easier the more you teach. Here are some general guidelines to guide you in this endeavor:

- ✓ Get a copy of the report card early in the year and become familiar with it. Emphasize report card objectives when planning your units and be sure you know how you will evaluate each objective.
- ✓ Assess students regularly rather than only close to the reporting period.
- ✓ Plan how you will assess each unit as you design each unit (not towards the end of the unit).
- ✓ Whenever possible, involve students in choosing the type of assessment.
- ✓ Be sure that your evaluation is authentic – does your assessment strategy truly assess what the students know?
- ✓ Be sure your evaluation reflects the current content that you are teaching.
- ✓ Do NOT try to assess everything! Be selective and choose only to evaluate student work that reflects benchmarks in learning.
- ✓ Keep in mind that you are evaluating students to help you to make informed decisions regarding future instruction.
- ✓ Remember that your goal is also to make students aware of their own strengths and weaknesses.
- ✓ Ask yourself – do your assessment methods have some value beyond your evaluation?

> "When people write letters, news articles, insurance claims, poems; when they speak a foreign language; when they develop blueprints; when they create a painting, a piece of music, or build a stereo cabinet, they demonstrate achievements that have special value missing in tasks contrived only for the purpose of assessing knowledge (such as spelling quizzes, laboratory exercises, or typical final exams)"
>
> (Archibald & Newman, 1988, p.3).

Three Types of Evaluation

There are three different types of evaluation that you should be aware of when planning assessment. These are defined by Burke (1994) as:

☆ **Diagnostic Evaluation**
This type of evaluation is often done at the beginning of a course, quarter, semester, or year to assess the skills, abilities, interests, levels of achievement, or difficulties of one student or a class. Diagnostic evaluation should be done informally; therefore, it should never be used for a grade.

☆ **Formative Evaluation**
These evaluations are conducted continually throughout the year. They are used to monitor students' progress and provide meaningful and immediate feedback as to what students have to do to achieve thoughtful outcomes; their purpose is to improve instruction rather than grade students.

☆ **Summative Evaluation**
"Summative evaluation occurs at the end of a unit, activity, course, term or program. It is used with formative evaluation to determine student achievement and program effectiveness" (Board of Education for the City of Etobicoke, 1987, p.9).

EVALUATION STRATEGIES

Authentic assessment means using a variety of evaluation strategies that are suited to your current topic of study. Here are some strategies available to you:

Standardized tests	Teacher-made tests
Portfolios	Performances
Projects	Oral exams
Peer Assessment	Exhibitions
Pre-tests	Essay style questions
Learning logs	Journals
Cloze activities	Miscue analysis
Observation checklists	Multiple choice
Short answer	Matching
Graphic organizers	Quizzes
Interviews	Homework checks
Anecdotal comments	Conferences
Author's chair	Take-home tests
Open book exams	Self-assessment
True or false	Self-reflection

★ Remember to consider the pros and cons of each type of evaluation. For example, multiple choice exams take a great deal of time to make, but very little time to mark, and may not authentically reflect what the student knows.

USING RUBRICS AS AN ASSESSMENT TOOL

The Alberta Assessment Consortium (August 1995 Draft 1.2) defines rubrics as "sets of criteria that describe levels of performance or understanding" (p.15). They are

- ✓ A set of criteria.
- ✓ A list of traits and qualities.
- ✓ Refer to the levels of understanding, proficiency with a skill or process, and/or the quality of a product or performance.

- ✓ Provides standards.
- ✓ Scales (2 or more levels) to help to differentiate levels of performance based on criteria.

Morris (2001) defines the rubric as "the ultimate assessment tool." She has found that the rubric:

> "simplifies assessment by providing a framework for teachers. Teachers can use it for both objective and subjective assessments (presentations, performances, and projects). The rubric provides a system for clearly assessing accountability. It is an authentic assessment tool that takes the guesswork out of evaluating student work. It is fast and efficient, and you can involve students in the development of the rubric through to the actual work assessment at the end of the unit" (p.51).

Here are some examples of rubrics to get you started:

4 Demonstrates <u>exemplary</u> performance or understanding. I.e.: higher level thinking skills such as inference and synthesis are applied.
3 Demonstrates *solid* performance or understanding.
2 Performance/understanding emerging or developing; makes errors; has a grasp that is not thorough.
1 Might attempt but has serious errors or misconceptions.

(Alberta Assessment Consortium, August 1995 Draft 1.2)

Some qualitative and quantitative descriptors are:

5	4	3	2	1
• Exceptional • Exemplary • Superior • Impressive • Excellent • Exceeds • Considerable • Advanced	• Above Gr. level • Above average • Consistent • Approaches excellence • Skillful • Approaching mastery • Proficient • Thorough	• At Gr. level • Average • Moderate • Adequate • Usually independent • Competent • Generally satisfactory • Usually consistent	• Sometimes adequate • Inconsistent • Somewhat • Slightly below • Minimal • Limited • Little • Few	• Insufficient • Very little • Requires attention • Not evident • No evidence • Incomplete • No attempt

CHAPTER 7:
ESTABLISHING POSITIVE PARENT RELATIONSHIPS

Some Helpful Tips

As a beginning teacher, the most intimidating moment for me was walking into a room of adults who had come to 'check out the new teacher'. It was daunting to ask them to become partners in their child's learning when I was younger than most of the parents! Couple this with the fact that beginning teachers have received little to no information on how to handle this situation, and it can be a very intimidating experience. Yet what I learned was that I was successful even before I opened my mouth to speak, because the approach I had taken to establishing my classroom and the relationships with my students and their parents spoke volumes for my professionalism. Parent involvement is fundamental to effective teaching, and the approach you take from the beginning of the year will in part determine how much support you will receive throughout the year. Here are some tips to get you off to a wonderful year!

Written communication with parents

You will be writing numerous letters to parents throughout the school year. It is important to maintain a positive, warm, professional, and respectful tone when communicating with the parents of your students. This is particularly true when taking into consideration online communication. With the rapid increase of email being used as a communication method the tendency is to fall into the trap of being too casual. Treat all written communication with peers, administration, and parents as a professional obligation. I have included illustrative examples of letters to parents in the Appendix, on pages a.61 to a.71, for you to use and modify to suit your own teaching context.

Meet the Teacher Night/Open House

Here is some information you may wish to share with your parents on this night:

- ☐ A letter from you (this could also be sent before school starts) including an introduction from you, telling a bit about your background, special events this year, and any other relevant information.
- ☐ Inform parents of exactly which classes you will be teaching along with your grading system.
- ☐ Your classroom daily/weekly schedule.
- ☐ When regular tests will occur (spelling, math) and how they can help their child to study.
- ☐ Your expectations regarding illness, absence, and homework.
- ☐ Offer suggestions on how parents can help at home.
- ☐ Your class rules and/or your management plan. On this plan, indicate when they would be receiving a phone call from you (for example, when their child has broken a rule 3 times in one week). Remember to also tell parents that you will also be phoning with POSITIVE comments on occasion (if you intend to do this).
- ☐ Information about breakfast/lunch programs available through the school.
- ☐ School supply list.
- ☐ Special upcoming field-trips/performances.
- ☐ Make up a schedule and ask for parent volunteers (name and phone number) during specific times for specific activities/subject areas, field trips, birthdays, and/or special occasions.
- ☐ Offer an invitation for parents as guest speakers for upcoming future units of study.
- ☐ Are parents allowed to drop in to observe your class? If so, is there a procedure they need to follow, such as checking in at the office?
- ☐ What do parents do if their child is having difficulty with you or with your class? Encourage parents not to wait until conference time if they feel there is a problem!
- ☐ Ask parents what they hope their child will accomplish this year! This one is very important. I will also often invite parents to write me a letter to tell me about their child at the beginning of the school year in order to let me know more about his/her likes and dislikes, personality, greatest strengths, etc.

☐ Other information: ______________________________

____

____

Here are some fun ways to get your classroom ready for this event!

- ☐ Play some soft music in the background.
- ☐ Provide some adult-sized chairs.
- ☐ Provide some toys for youngsters to play with who come with their older brothers and sisters.
- ☐ Have a sign-in sheet for parents, or a table covered with butcher paper where parents can comment on your classroom (by writing right on the table!)
- ☐ Have the children put their names on their desks or make desk cards with your students.
- ☐ Have the children write a letter to their parents or make a card to thank them for coming, to tell them what they've learned, or what (s)he likes most about school, and include a schedule of events or topics you will be covering that evening.
- ☐ Put other student work on desks in folders for students to show parents.
- ☐ Have the students give their parents a tour of their classroom, or design a short scavenger hunt for students to do with their parents. For example, "Find the reading corner and write down the temperature" The students who finish can come to you to be rewarded with a sticker.
- ☐ Have the parents sit in their children's desks. At each child's desk have one question you think the parents might want to ask or have answered by you. Alternatively, you could have the children answer the questions (you would need to plan this carefully before hand).
- ☐ Have the children write three clues that describe themselves and leave them on their desks for their parents to find that evening.
- ☐ Have your bulletin boards decorated with student work.

Maintaining Positive Relationships Throughout the year

- ☐ Make a point of phoning all of your parents to introduce yourself and ask if there is any important information that you should know about their child: for example, nick-names, allergies, etc.
- ☐ Keep file cards with positive things that happen on them, and then send postcards or happy-grams home with positive remarks. Send one or two per day.
- ☐ Make a habit of sending home weekly or monthly newsletters, either student or teacher generated.

- ☐ Send corrected work home regularly and on a timely basis. In my classroom, each child has a manila envelope which their work goes home in, to be signed and returned the next day.
- ☐ Send home positive praise for good work the first few weeks of school in the form of a small progress report – something for students to take home and brag about! This could also be in the form of a checklist for parents to sign and return.
- ☐ Take pictures of your students doing various different activities in your classroom. Have students write captions for each photo and bind in an album. Students can take turns bringing this home for the weekend!
- ☐ Throughout the year, invite parents to come in to listen to individual children read, particularly for those children who rarely have the opportunity to have someone listen to them at home.
- ☐ Provide each child with a chart with space for 20 stickers. Again, I have provided one for you in the Appendix on page a.76. Reward positive Behavior/good work with a sticker. When the student has filled his/her chart, they earn the privilege of inviting mom and/or dad to school for lunch. Set up a table complete with a vase of flowers in a corner of your room for this purpose (parents bring the lunch). After lunch, the student can give mom and dad a tour of the classroom or show them current work!

Home Communication Books and Class Auctions

Classroom auctions are one of my favorite ways to reward students in a positive way for choosing to be responsible citizens in my classroom, and they are also a wonderful way to establish and maintain daily contact with parents. I usually hold two class auctions each year. The first auction is held at the end of January and the second at the end of June.

In my classroom, my students are required to write in a Home Communication Book each day after lunch as part of their afternoon routine. The Home Communication Book is a form of home/school communication so that I can help to keep parents informed about what is happening at school, and so the parents can keep me updated about important information such as needing to miss school for an appointment. Each day that the child brings their Home Communication Book back to school initialled by their guardian, I also initial to indicate that I have seen their book.

At the end of each week, if a student has earned a minimum of four initials by both me and by his or her parent, the student receives one 'scholar dollar' (play money) to keep in his or her 'account' (which is a paper envelope taped firmly to the inside of the child's agenda). If a child loses his or her envelope of scholar dollars, we hold a class meeting to determine how the situation should be handled. Usually the class agrees to replace the scholar dollars the first time a child loses them. I have never had a child lose their scholar dollars more than once! To make this activity more challenging for students in upper elementary, I usually give the students their weekly 'scholar dollar' in the form of coins (i.e. four quarters, ten dimes, or a combination of quarters, dimes, and nickels).

During the auctions, the children are able to spend the "money" they have earned from bringing their communication books to and from school on a regular basis. This is a very valuable activity as it teaches children money skills while they earn positive rewards for being responsible. The items up for bid during the auction are a combination of items donated by parents, gift certificates designed by myself, or small items I come across at the dollar store throughout the year. Examples of some of these items include:

Auction Items:	**Certificates:**
Small stuffed animals	No spelling homework for one week
Bag of popcorn	Chew gum in class for a day (include gum)
Lip gloss	Pizza lunch with Mrs. Friesen
Markers	One jumbo freezie
Gel pens	Write in gel pen for the day
Hockey cards	Bring a stuffed animal to school for the day
Fancy erasers	Sit where you choose for the day
Fancy pencils	15 minutes of free time (not during a test)
Slinky	Sit in Mrs. Friesen's desk for the day
Stickers	
Surprise Bags (teacher made)	
Skipping ropes	
Small toys/cars	

I will usually put the items up for bid on display on a table at the front of the room, and ask that students to fill out a sheet indicating which items they are planning to bid for (a copy of this is in the Appendix). The students keep these on their desk during the auction so that during the event, my parent volunteers and I can keep track of what has been purchased by whom. To run this event, I usually ask for three parent volunteers:

- ✓ one parent to ensure that each child has bid for and 'won' something (subtle gestures between myself and the parent usually takes care of this)
- ✓ one parent to help children count out their money before we begin and again after they have bought something
- ✓ one parent to actually take the scholar dollars and record the items which have been purchased on a master sheet (included in the Appendix). This is a very helpful record of which items were most popular for this class when planning the second auction.

The only rules during the auction are the following:

1. At least one part of the students' body must be touching their desk.
2. No standing on your seat is allowed.
3. You must go up in one dollar increments when bidding on an item.

I have had nothing but positive feedback from both parents and students in my classroom when I run this event. In fact, when I ask the students at the end of the year what their favorite part was, the "Great Class Auction" is always listed among the highlights. What a fun way to teach students responsibility while maintaining close contact with their parents! I have included my letter to parents, a student planning page, and gift certificate and thank-you note templates for parents for your use in the Appendix on pages a.70 to a.75.

Parent – Teacher Conferences

Although your first round of parent-teacher interviews may seem daunting, remember that there is no enemy here! You are both on the same side, concerned about the wellbeing and educational growth of their child. Some parents seem to come into parent-teacher conferences unsure or upset, perhaps due to their own negative memories of school, or because they are afraid that their child's educational problems are their own fault. Nonetheless, it is important to remain calm, professional, and positive.

> "Parents are a powerful, usually underutilised source of knowledge about youngsters. Parents are often made to feel unwelcome in schools, and we too often dismiss their insights as too subjective and overly involved. In fact, the insights of parents – urgent, invested, passionate, immediate – are exactly what we need"
>
> (Ayers, 1993, p.41)

Prior to the Conference

- ☐ Send home list of questions the parent might want to ask. Please see the Appendix for an example.
- ☐ Determine whether or not the student will be present at the conference.
- ☐ Review the student's cumulative file. Students' home lives and background are helpful to know.
- ☐ If you are aware that a student's parents do not speak English, arrange for an interpreter.
- ☐ If you feel that you will need administrative support for a particular conference, arrange for this in advance with your principal.
- ☐ On an index card, in a binder, or on a file folder, list in point form:
  - ☆ 1 or 2 positive qualities about the student
  - ☆ 1 or 2 goals for this term/semester
  - ☆ Be sure this is supported by current samples of the student's work from his/her portfolio or file.

  * I have included a "Report Card Comments" form in the Appendix, on page a.77, for you to modify/adapt to your own teaching style and report card.

- ☐ If you wish, collect student notebooks/binders and put them on display in the hallway for the students to show parents while waiting. I have my parents come 15 minutes early for their interview for this purpose. Note: To protect the privacy of your students, place all work in a sealed envelope just prior to the interview, and have parents bring all work back into the classroom with them when they come in for the interview.
- ☐ If you anticipate that a certain child may need longer time than the scheduled interview, prearrange to have the interview at a different time.
- ☐ Also put on display any relevant current research you have come across regarding student learning in relevant curriculum areas.
- ☐ Have parents help themselves to a copy of a current newsletter outlining topics of study and upcoming events.
- ☐ All appointments and your name should be clearly marked on the outside of your door. I also post a sign asking parents to knock if it is their scheduled time. This helps me to keep track of time, and I can either wrap up or schedule a second interview for the parent who requests more time.

Setting the Stage

The atmosphere in which you set up parent-teacher conferences should be welcoming and professional. Keep these tips in mind:

- ✓ An empty classroom, free of distractions, is best.
- ✓ Be sure the time and place of the conference is clear to both you and the parent.
- ✓ Do not sit across from the parent(s) with furniture between you such as a desk – sit side by side on adult chairs at equal height.
- ✓ If possible, offer refreshments such as coffee/juice and mints or cookies in the hallway.
- ✓ Provide books and toys for young children accompanying parents to play with.
- ✓ Consider putting a plant or some fresh flowers on the table with a bright tablecloth.

During the Conference

- ✓ Be prepared to listen.
- ✓ Greet the parents/student at the door with a warm welcome and smile.
- ✓ Open with a positive comment about the student's attitude, work habits, or achievements.
- ✓ Stay open to hearing the parent first. Avoid rushing in to defend your practice. Display clarity and confidence in your own philosophy and classroom practice.
- ✓ Be open to suggestions and to working together. Ask for the parent's perception of their child's strengths and weaknesses before offering yours.
- ✓ Remain sensitive to what the parent is feeling.
- ✓ Remain positive with both your words and your body language.
- ✓ Speak plainly and avoid the use of educational jargon.
- ✓ Discuss the child's:
  - ☆ Educational progress
  - ☆ Social skills
  - ☆ Work habits
  - ☆ Emotional growth
  - ☆ Physical health (if necessary)
- ✓ When discussing Behavior problems and educational issues, stick to the facts. Support what you are saying with specific incidents and/or work samples.

- ✓ Keep writing to a minimum during the interview, but keep brief notes about what was discussed.
- ✓ Stay on schedule! Parents may have other interviews scheduled for siblings of the child in your class, or other appointments to be at.
- ✓ If a parent becomes verbally abusive, stop the conference and arrange to meet at a different date (with administrative support if necessary).

Concluding the Conference

Here are some final things to do when the conference ends.

- ☐ Summarize the important topics of discussion. Reflect parents' statements back to them and do further inquiry if necessary.
- ☐ Establish goals for the next term (no more than 3) and give parents a copy.
- ☐ Review the plan of action to be sure everyone (including you), understands and agrees.
- ☐ Ask parents if they have any further concerns.
- ☐ End with another positive comment about the student.
- ☐ Thank the parents (and the student) for coming and for their continued support.
- ☐ Write short anecdotal notes once the parents leave (if possible!) to remind you of further plans of action.
- ☐ Add any items to your "Post-Conference To Do List" to remind you of follow-up after the conference, including extra work/support/enrichment to be sent home, student/teacher contracts, phone calls, referrals, etc.

CHAPTER 8: SURVIVAL

TIPS FOR PREVENTING STRESS

Here are some words of wisdom I have been taught along the way of my own beginning career. This may sound like a cliche, but you are no good inside the classroom if you aren't taking care of yourself outside of the classroom. Please, be sure to:

- ✓ Learn how not to be a perfectionist.
- ✓ Get enough sleep.
- ✓ Watch what you eat. Eat plenty of high energy, nutritious foods. Pack your lunch the night before and keep a stash of healthy snacks in your classroom for YOU, not for the students! Keep low fat granola bars, power bars and fresh fruit on hand at all times.
- ✓ Drink plenty of water. It's easy to fall into the trap of drinking 5 cups of coffee a day!
- ✓ If you get sick, STAY HOME! Beginning teachers especially seem to have this belief that they simply can't miss a day or everything will fall apart. Take the time to allow your body to heal itself or you will never fully recover.
- ✓ Try not to do too much in your first year. You simply cannot expect to have fully developed units completed for each topic the first time that you teach them! Choose one subject to develop fully your first year, and another for the next. Your administrator will discuss this with you as well. Be gentle with yourself.
- ✓ Continue to exercise. Plan this as religiously as you would the classes you teach.
- ✓ Leave your work problems at work and your home problems at home. Easier said than done sometimes, but very good advice.

- ✓ Laugh at yourself! You're going to make some pretty silly mistakes this year. When you crash into the filing cabinet or knock over the book display, remember that you can teach a valuable lesson to your students by learning to take mistakes in stride.
- ✓ Keep a clean desk. Psychologically, this may help you to keep a clear mind.
- ✓ Worry only about things that are under your control or that you can change.
- ✓ Maintain your personal interests outside of the classroom. The most popular reward in my class, and the one that gets the attention of the one child who doesn't seem to care about anything, is the offer of one of my travel stories. I have a growing list of the countries I've been to, and the 'best worker in the class' gets to choose which country I'll tell a story about. I love to tell them because I am talking about my passion, and I am appearing more 'real' to my students who someday may wish to travel themselves.

When You've Had 'One of Those Days'

We've all had them, those days when nothing seems to go right, when the lessons we've worked so hard to create flopped miserably or we've had a negative run-in with someone in the building despite our very best efforts. You are not alone, and it does not mean that you are not a good teacher. This is a natural part of the roller coaster of emotions experienced by beginning teachers. Here's what you need to do:

- ✓ Talk to other beginning teachers. Go out for coffee together and discuss your concerns. (But be careful to adhere to privacy legislation here!)
- ✓ Write in a journal. I keep a journal and always seem to turn to it when I need to work through a problem. It is amazing what I learn about myself as a teacher from re-reading previous experiences.
- ✓ Talk to your mentor. Ask a dozen questions!
- ✓ Indulge yourself. Whatever you do to help yourself relax, do it. Go for a nice, long walk, take a bubble bath, get a massage, meditate.
- ✓ When stress begins to mount, take 5 minute breaks either mentally or physically. Close your eyes and escape to another place in your mind, or take a short walk on your lunch break. Taking 5 or 10 minutes alone in my classroom listening to music at lunch was an absolute for me during my first year!
- ✓ Focus on your strengths and on your successes. Write these down in a journal and read them when you are feeling low.

- ✓ Write down one of the many positive incidents that have happened in your classroom or things that make you laugh in a special book that will bring you a smile when you are down.
- ✓ Keep special notes/pictures/positive letters from students, parents, and those you love in an envelope to leaf through when you need a pick-me-up.
- ✓ Let yourself cry. We've all been there, and it does get better.

Chapter 9: A Fantastic Finish!

Making the Last Month of School Memorable

Phew – you are almost there! June can be a challenging month in so many ways. Often, the children (and of course, yourself) are tired by this time of the year and there are many distractions outside of the classroom that can take away from your students' focus. Embrace all that the upcoming summer has to offer in your June planning and you will be guaranteed a wonderful finish. Here are some of my favorite ideas of how to ensure a fabulous finish to your year:

Classroom Graffiti and Book Talks

One of my favorite ways to wrap up the year is by spending some time remembering and honoring our favorite books. First, as a class, we brainstorm as many book titles as we can from our year. We then cover an entire wall of our classroom with a giant sheet of butcher paper, and using large, fat, colorful markers, the students write down as many book titles and authors as they can remember all over the paper. We leave the butcher paper up for a few days so that students can write down more book titles as they remember them. I then ask the students to choose one book that they would like to read aloud to the class. If it is a picture book they love, they are invited to read the entire book. If it is a chapter book, I encourage the students to either read the first chapter or their favorite chapter from the book. The students are then given about a week to practice reading their book and are also asked to fill out a 'planning sheet' for their book talk (Appendix, page a.79). The planning sheet is a great way for the students to prepare for their reading, to help them to think about what they want the class to notice about the book, and why they chose this book in particular. Doing book talks in this way also gives the students an opportunity to practice public speaking and gives me an idea of their growth in this area through this type of performance assessment. After students have chosen a book, they then sign up for a date and, on that day, they present their book to the class. I usually schedule 2-3 book talks per day – one first thing in the morning, another for after lunch or recess, and one to end the day. Because many of the books chosen are class favorites, this is a wonderful way for the students to revisit popular authors and, of course, great books are meant to be read again and again! The element of choice is a great motivator for this activity, and it gives me as a teacher further insight into the level my students are comfortable with in their independent reading. What a fun and meaningful way to end the year!

Letters to Next Year's Class

One of my favorite activities to do in the last week of school is to ask my students to write a letter to my next years' class. This is a great way for me to gain some insight into what my students thought about their time in our classroom and to understand how they are feeling about this experience. Depending on the age and ability of your students, you may wish to use the template included in the Appendix on page a.78, or encourage students to write their own letters. Some topics you may request your students address include discussing what the children think the new students will enjoy about this grade, what their favorite subjects and/or projects were and why they enjoyed them, and advice for how to succeed in their new classroom. On the first day of school the following year, my new students are then each given a letter from a past student in my class.

A Meaningful Ending: Class Yearbooks

If you have been gathering student work samples throughout the year already for student portfolios, a Class Yearbook is a wonderful final chapter to add to them before students leave your classroom. We usually work on our yearbooks in the last two to three weeks of school as they are a wonderfully meaningful and engaging language arts project. I have included in the Appendix, on pages a.82 to a.91, a page for each of the topics we usually include in our yearbooks:

- ✓ the funniest thing that happened this year
- ✓ the best book(s) I read this year
- ✓ some of my best friends this year
- ✓ all about my classmates
- ✓ "Time Stands Still" – my favorites: food, hobbies, etc.

- ✓ ways I have changed this year
- ✓ a birds' eye view of our classroom
- ✓ what I love about our school playground
- ✓ my favorite field trip this year
- ✓ special occasions I always want to remember
- ✓ the subject I enjoyed the most
- ✓ one thing I'll always remember about my teacher
- ✓ something I'm really proud of from this year
- ✓ autographs (from classmates, teachers, and other adults from the school)
- ✓ student-generated ideas!

I usually write each of these topics on cards (also included in the Appendix for your use) and hold them up like playing cards. I then invite a student to "choose a card, any card," and the class will then do the yearbook page selected by the student. Of course, this means that you need to be very organized and have all yearbook pages copied and ready to go! Alternatively, you may want to just pick and choose which activity pages suit your teaching style and context – you know your students best!

Gifts to End the Year

Students love to give their teachers gifts at the end of the year, but it was always difficult for me to decide what to give to my students as my final gift to them. The gifts that are the most meaningful are those which come from your heart, and it is in this spirit of giving that I offer the following ideas.

Teacher-Made Bookmarks – One gift I love to give to my students are bookmarks with a meaningful message from me, or I will have the students all sign a bookmark for each child as a memento of who was in their class that year. I usually print these in colour, laminate them and give one to each student, along with a copy of a favorite book (if I can find a great sale!). I have included templates for two of these bookmarks in the Appendix, on pages a.80 and a.81, titled "101 Ways to Say You're Wonderful" and "Never Forget . . ."

Messages from the Heart – At the end of the school year I always remind my students how much they mean to me by giving each child a special message. One of my favorite ways to do this is with a poster titled "You are So Special" to remind each child of their own uniqueness in this world. When our class fell in love with the game, "Who Wants to Be a Millionaire?" I designed a card for each of my students which read "You are Worth a Million . . . To Me", and included an imitation million dollar bill in each child's card. I have included copies of both ideas for you in the Appendix, on pages a.92 to a.93, for use with your own students!

Homemade CD's or DVD's – probably one of my favorite ideas for a gift to my students at the end of the year is a CD filled with memories of our year together. Throughout the year as our class participates in special projects, field trips, and special occasions, I take digital photos and store them in folders on my computer. If our class does any drama presentations, puppet plays, or other dramatic events, I also include videos of these events. At the end of the year, it's simply a matter of burning all of these pictures onto a CD and making enough copies for each of my students. I then make each child a CD cover (usually with a photo of each child from their first day of school, or a class photo) and Table of Contents. On the last day of school, I arrange for a projector to be set up in our classroom, and our class watches all of the photos from the year as part of our class party. I then give each child their own copy of the CD in their report cards. What a wonderful way to end the year and to preserve precious memories of our time together! I have included a copy of my CD cover, along with a sample Table of Contents for your use in the Appendix on pages a.94 to a.95.

Here are some ideas of topics you may want to include on your own CD:

- ✓ First Day of Grade ____
- ✓ Our Teachers
- ✓ Halloween
- ✓ Christmas
- ✓ Our Great Grade __ Auction
- ✓ 100th Day of School
- ✓ Book Buddies
- ✓ Our Field Trip to ______________
- ✓ Valentine's Day
- ✓ Easter
- ✓ Class Puppet Plays
- ✓ Sports Day
- ✓ Swimming

Thank You to Parents

How do you say thank you to parents who have volunteered in your classroom, been available to drive students for field trips, and supported your efforts this year? One idea that costs virtually no money at all is to make up certificates of thanks. Many teachers I know have made "thumbs up" certificates, and then have the students put their thumbprint onto the certificate in ink. What a creative and meaningful way to say thank you! One version of this certificate is included for you in the Appendix on page a.96; feel free to adapt it for your own use.

REFERENCES

Alberta Learning (1986). *Behavior disorders in schools: A practical guide to identification, assessment, and correction.* Alberta Education, Special Education Services.

Alberta Learning (2000). *Teaching students who are gifted and talented: Programming for students with special needs.* Alberta Learning, Special Education Branch.

Alberta Education (1996). *Teaching students with learning disabilities.* Alberta Education, Special Education Branch.

Alberta Learning (2002). *Unlocking potential: Key Components of Programming for Students with Learning Disabilities.* Alberta Learning, Learning and Teaching Resources Branch.

Archibald, D.A., & Newman, F.M. (1988). *Beyond standardized testing: Assessing authentic achievement in the secondary school.* Madison: University of Wisconsin, National Association of Secondary School Principals.

Ayers, W. (1993). *To teach: The journey of a teacher.* New York: Teachers College Press.

Alberta Teachers' Association. (2001). *Beginning teachers' handbook.* Edmonton, AB: Alberta Teachers' Association.

Badali, S. J. (1996). One year later: Beginning teachers revisit their preparation program experiences. *Alberta Journal of Educational Research, 42* (4), 378-395.

Black, S. (2004). Helping teachers helps keep them around. *Education Digest, 70*, (4), 46-51.

Boe, E.E. & Shin, S. (2007). Does teacher preparation matter for beginning teachers in either special or general education? *The Journal of Special Education, 41*, (3), 158-170.

Board of Education for the City of Etobicoke. (1987). *Making the grade: Evaluating student progress.* Scarborough, ON: Prentice-Hall Canada.

Burke, K. (1994). *The mindful school: How to assess authentic learning.* Arlington Heights, IL: IRI/Skylight Training and Publishing.

Darling-Hammond, L. (2003). Keeping good teachers: Why it matters, what leaders can do. *Educational Leadership, 59*, (6). Retrieved November 11, 2007, from Academic Search Premier database.

Darling-Hammond, L, Chung, R. & Frelow, F. (2002). Variation in teacher preparation: How well do different pathways prepare teachers to teach? *Journal of Teacher Education, 53*, (4), 286-302. Retrieved November 4, 2007 from http://jte.sagepub.com/cgi/content/abstract/53/4/286.

Dollase, R. H. (1992). *Voices of beginning teachers: Visions and realities.* New York, N.Y.: Teachers College Press.

Emmer, Edmund, Evertson, Clements, & Worsham (1997). *Classroom management for secondary teachers* (3rd ed). Needham Heights, Mass.: Allyn & Bacon.

Evertson, C., Emmer, E, Clements, B., & Worsham, M. (1994). *Classroom management for elementary teachers.* Needham Heights, MASS.: Allyn & Bacon.

Frieberg, J. H. (2002). Essential skills for new teachers. *Educational Leadership, 59*, (6), 56-60. Retrieved November 4, 2007, from Academic Search Premier database.

Gardner, H. (1983). *Frames of mind: The theory of multiple intelligences.* New York, NY: Basic.

Good, T. L. & Brophy, J.E. (1997). *Looking in classrooms*, 7th ed. New York, NY: Harper and Row.

Henke, R.R., Chen, X., & Geis, S. (2000). *Progress through the teacher pipeline: 1992-93 college graduates and elementary/secondary school teaching as of 1997.* Washington, DC: National Center of Education Statistics.

Housego, B.E.J. (1994). How Prepared Were You to Teach? Beginning Teachers Assess Their Preparedness. *The Alberta Journal of Educational Research, 40*, (3), 355-373.

Idaho State Department of Education. Teacher Education and Certification. (1994) *Beginning educator handbook: A resource for first year educators.* Idaho State Department of Education.

IMPACT II – The Teachers Network. (1991). *New teachers handbook.* 2nd Ed. Mechaniesburg, Pennsylvania: Fry Communication.

Ingersoll, R.M. & Smith, T.M. (2003). The wrong solution to the teacher shortage. *Educational Leadership, 60*, (8), 30-33. Retrieved November 4, 2007, from EBSCOhost database.

Jonson, K. F. (1997). *The new elementary teacher's handbook: (Almost) everything you need to know for your first years of teaching.* Thousand Oaks, CA: Corwin Press.

Johnson, S.M. & Birkeland, S.E. (2003). Pursuing a "Sense of success": New teachers explain their career decisions. *American Educational Research Journal, 40*, (3), 581-617.

Johnson, S.M. & Kardos, S.M. (2002). Keeping new teachers in mind. *Educational Leadership, 59*, (6), 12-16. Retrieved November 4, 2007 from Academic Search Premier database.

Kardos, S.M, Johnson, S.M., Peske, H.G., Kauffman, D., & Liu, E. (2001). Counting on colleagues: New teachers encounter the professional cultures of their schools. *Educational Administration Quarterly, 37*, (2), 250-290.

Lundy, K. G. (2004). *What do I do about the kid who…?* Markham, Ontario: Pembroke.

Lynn, K. (2001). *Alphabet soup: A primer for beginning teachers.* US Department of Education, Office of Educational Research and Improvement.

MacDonald, R. E. & Healy, S.D. (1999). *A handbook for beginning teachers*: Second edition. New York, NY: Addison Wesley Longman.

Mazur, A. (2007). Can I give you a hug? *English Journal*, *96*, (6), 14-15. Retrieved November 27, 2007, from Academic Search Premier database.

Merseth, K. K. (1992). First aid for first year teachers. *Phi Delta Kappan*, *73*, (9), 678-83.

Metropolitan Nashville Education Association (MNEA). (1987, August). *New teachers' handbook*. Nashville, TN: Author.

Morris, T. (2001). *101 time smart solutions for teachers*. Winnipeg, MN: Portage & Main Press.

Nemser, S. F. (2003). What new teachers need to learn. *Educational Leadership: Association for Supervision and Curriculum Development*, *60*, (8), 25-29. Retrieved November 4, 2007, from Academic Search Premier database.

Nielbrand, C., Horn, E., & Holmes, R. (1992). Insecurity, confusion: Common complaints of the first year teacher. *NASSP Bulletin*, *76*, (546), 84-89.

O'Connell Rust, F. (1994). The first year of teaching: It's not what they expected. *Teaching and Teacher Education*, *10*, (2), 205-217.

Romano, M. & Gibson, P. (2006). Beginning teacher successes and struggles: An elementary teacher's reflections on the first year of teaching. *The Professional Educator*, *2*, (1). Retrieved November 28, 2007 from Academic Search Premier database.

Renard, L. (2003). Setting new teachers up for failure . . . or success. *Educational Leadership*, *60*, (8), 62-64. Retrieved November 4, 2007, from EBSCOhost database.

Sargent, B. (2003). Finding good teachers – and keeping them. *Educational Leadership*, *60*, (8), 44-47. Retrieved November 4, 2007, from EBSCOhost database.

Schell, L. M. & Burden, P.R. (1982). *Before school starts: A handbook for the inexperienced elementary school teacher*. Paper Presented at the Fourth Annual Rural and Small Schools Conference, College of Education. Kansas State University, Manhattan, KS.

Steele, A.L. (1999). *Multiple intelligences: Teaching kids the way they learn*. Torrance, CA: Frank Schaffer Publications.

Stipek, D. J. (1988). *Motivation to learn: From theory to practice*. Englewood Cliffs, NJ: Prentice-Hall.

Stone, R. (2005). *Best classroom management practices for reaching all learners*. Thousand Oaks, California: Corwin.

Tellez, K. (1992). Mentors By Choice, Not Design: Help-Seeking by Beginning Teachers. *The Journal of Teacher Education*, *43*, (3), 214-21.

Tennessee Education Association Appalachia Educational Library. (1988). *Bridges to strength: The TEA-AEL beginning teacher's handbook*. Washington, DC: Tenesse Education Association & Appalachia Educational Library.

Veenman, S. (1984). Perceived problems of beginning teachers. *Review of Educational Research*, *54*, 143-78.

Wong, H.K. & Wong, R.T. (1998). *The first days of school*. Mountain View, CA: Harry K. Wong Publications.

APPENDIX

The following Appendix contains various templates and sample activities that I've used in my own classroom. I've included them here to serve as a starting point for the development of your own ideas and activities for use in your classroom. It's important that you consider your own context and adapt any of these templates to suit your own teaching style and instructional needs.

This Appendix is design to allow you to peruse these templates and find the ones that work best for you. After making any changes you would like, you can then print off full-sized colour documents from the disc provided with this book. To make the documents on the disc easier to navigate, the page numbers in this Appendix match the page numbers of the documents in the Microsoft Word© file (i.e. a.34 in the Appendix is page 34 in the document).

Please note: The documents in this Appendix contain clipart protected under the licensing agreement for Microsoft Word©. Under this agreement, these documents can be distributed within a classroom for educational use. Please ensure that you or the school own a licensed version of Word before distributing these documents.

Contents of Appendix

Preparation for the First Day (Chapter 1)

Activities for the First Day of School (Chapter 2)

Getting-To-Know-You Activities (Chapter 3)

TEMPLATES/ACTIVITIES FOR CLASSROOM MANAGEMENT (CHAPTER 4)

TEMPLATES FOR PARENT/TEACHER COMMUNICATION (CHAPTER 7)

END OF THE YEAR ACTIVITIES (CHAPTER 9)

GENERAL-USE CHECKLISTS

Sample Beginning of the Year Newsletter

Monday, September 9, 2002

Welcome Grade Four Parents and Students,

I hope that you had a wonderful summer! Here are a few items of information about the grade 4 program and expectations you may wish to know.

Mr. Legg teaches science to all three grade 4 classes.

Mrs. Goertz teaches all of the grade 4 French classes. She also teaches a modified language arts program for selected students.

Mr. Bakke teaches the grade 4 social studies.

Mrs. Fender teaches all of the grade 4 art.

Mr. High teaches all of the grade 4 music.

Mathematics - The course is heavy and the children are able to progress much more rapidly if they have their basic facts memorized. Our goal is to memorize the addition and subtraction facts by the end of November. We will then spend the time necessary to memorize the multiplication facts (probably 3 or 4 months). At that point, we will start on the division facts. Although the children will practice these facts at school, your continued support in this area at home is greatly appreciated through the use of flash cards.

Reading - The children need to continue daily reading at home supervised by an adult. Supervision may be no more than providing a quiet time and place, or it may be much more intensive, with the adult sitting down and listening to the child read aloud. At school we read a variety of genres, and I would encourage you to supply a variety of reading materials at home. This could include magazines, newspapers, poetry, mystery novels, etc.

Writing - The children learn/review cursive writing this year, and after Christmas, many assignments will be done entirely in cursive writing.

Composition - In grade 4, the children will write autobiographies, fiction, friendly letters, formal letters, poetry, narrative stories, photo essays, and fantasy stories, and learn the basics of note-taking using point form.

Social Studies - Grade four concentrates on Alberta; it's geography, resources, and history, and features a comparison with the province of Quebec. Research is an important skill here and is developed throughout these units.

Science - The units we study are Waste in Our World, Wheels and Levers, Building Devices That Move, Light and Shadows, and Plant Growth.

Miscellaneous - Please label all supplies and outdoor clothing.
- Library day is Wednesday.
- Spelling lists go home on Monday to be studied for a Friday test.

Thank you in advance for all of your support, and we look forward to a fun and rewarding year in grade four. Please don't hesitate to contact us should you have any further questions or concerns.

Sincerely,

The Grade Four Teachers

Our Class Newsletter

Look What's Happening This Month!	
Upcoming Events	Special Projects
Just a Reminder...	

Division One

Home Reading Program

Dear Parents,

Our home reading program will be run as follows:

Each day, your child will bring home two books (or one chapter book) in a Ziploc bag to read. Please write down in the blue half-scribbler the name of every book s/he reads (include personal and library books as well as the ones s/he brings home from school), and number them. The children will receive a sticker on our class sticker chart for every ten books they read at home. Certificates, bookmarks, and books will be awarded to children who reach their monthly reading goal of 40 books/month. Please return the bag to school **every morning**. I will exchange the books that day and send home new ones. **Reading EVERY night is top priority!** This will encourage the students to read more and increase their chances of success this year. Thank you so much for your commitment to this program and for your assistance in carrying it out!

Sincerely,

____

Mrs. A. Chinn

Division Two

Home Reading Program

Dear Parents,

Welcome back to school. I hope you and your family had a great summer. To get the year started off on the right foot, I would like to begin an at home reading program. Students are asked to continually read at home throughout the year. Depending on the student, they do not necessarily need to do <u>all</u> the reading. You may wish to take turns or you can perhaps read to your child. Whichever you choose, encourage your child to read, read, read. The practice will pay great dividends in all subject areas!

☺ <u>Some Suggestions</u> ☺

1. **Let your child choose reading material that they are interested in.** You may want to encourage them to read a variety of types of literature. Some examples include newspapers, poetry, comics, magazines, and notes from you. Also encourage your child to read chapter books of varied genres, such as mystery, fiction, autobiographies, and biographies.

2. **Ensure the reading material is of the appropriate reading level.** The "Five Finger Rule" seems to work well. Students choose a book and turn to a random page of text. They begin to read it aloud, and every time they encounter an unknown word, they put down a finger. If five fingers are down and they're still on the same page, the book is too difficult for them. If a book is too difficult, it will only create frustration. Let's build on successes!

3. **Set a regular time each day to read.** A thirty minute block of time may be enough (hopefully the children will soon say it's not long enough!). During that time, mix things up. Have them read silently, out loud, or listen to you read.

4. **This time will provide you with a time to read as well!** Be a role model. If children see you read, they will have a greater desire to read as well.

5. **Discuss the things you read about**. What a great way to stimulate conversation! Believe it or not, reading can become a very interactive family activity!

☺The Reading Record Sheet☺

A very important part of the reading program is record keeping. At the conclusion of each book (or other reading material), students will fill out and return a "Reading Record Sheet". This way, children will be able to enjoy and respond to reading material together. (It is not meant to be 'busy work', but a wonderful opportunity to concentrate on writing skills in conjunction with reading!). The information from this sheet will then be stored in your child's file to create individual reading profiles.

☺ **READING RECORD SHEET** ☺	
Student Name:	Date:
Title of Reading Material:	
Type of Material:	No. of Pages:
About the Book:	
Rating: 1 2 3 4 5 6 7 8 9 10	Parent Signature:

The Reading Record Sheet is quite self-explanatory. However, I would like to comment on a few sections:

Type of Material

In this space, indicate if the reading material was a book, comic, magazine, etc. If it was a book, what kind was it? Drama, mystery, joke, non-fiction, etc.

About the Book

In this space, your child writes a brief response to the selection. For example, what was your favourite part? What was something that bothered you? Why did you like/not like the selection? If you were the author, what would you change? Did you correctly guess who committed the crime? This is a very open category, with endless possibilities. Encourage your child to write a different kind of response for each selection they read!

Rating

In this small space, indicate on a scale of 1 to 10 (one being the worst, and ten being the best), how you would rate the selection. If you felt the selection was outstanding, give it a ten! If it was the pits, give it a one!

Parent Signature

I don't want the parents to feel left out! You're an invaluable part of the overall process.

Other

STUDENTS are to fill out the Reading Record Sheet, NOT parents! (Except for the parent signature, of course!).

If a student reads a number of 'longer' stories in one book, they may fill out a sheet for each story. They may also fill out a sheet if a book was read to them, or if it was a 'shared reading' with their parents or another member of the family.

Thank you in advance for your cooperation with this program. The final goal is to develop a love of reading, and all the joys that it can bring! As S.I. Hayakawa notes, "It is not true that we have only one life to live. If we read, we can live as many more lives and as many kinds of lives as we wish".

Happy Reading,

____

Ms. A. Grant
Grade 4 Teacher

☺ READING RECORD SHEET ☺	
Student Name:	Date:
Title of Reading Material:	
Type of Material:	No. of Pages:
About the Book:	
Rating: 1 2 3 4 5 6 7 8 9 10	Parent Signature:

☺ READING RECORD SHEET ☺	
Student Name:	Date:
Title of Reading Material:	
Type of Material:	No. of Pages:
About the Book:	
Rating: 1 2 3 4 5 6 7 8 9 10	Parent Signature:

Summer Fun Word Search

I	N	B	H	E	N	O	I	T	A	E	R	C	E	R
B	U	H	I	K	I	T	R	A	V	E	L	L	H	E
A	F	N	A	S	U	N	S	H	I	N	E	E	I	C
L	J	M	S	U	P	Y	G	P	A	R	H	M	K	R
L	U	E	R	P	G	L	Y	N	S	O	E	O	I	E
A	L	D	S	A	O	U	W	A	I	R	A	P	N	P
B	N	A	T	M	W	J	S	P	I	H	T	C	G	A
E	E	N	R	N	I	C	H	T	I	Y	S	O	U	R
S	C	O	O	U	T	D	O	O	R	B	M	I	A	K
A	I	M	P	S	E	B	A	L	Y	I	W	A	F	C
B	T	E	S	P	L	A	Y	R	W	M	S	O	C	I
W	S	L	I	N	E	C	T	S	U	M	M	E	R	N
I	L	S	U	N	M	I	R	E	C	C	O	S	O	C
M	O	T	U	R	I	N	S	E	C	T	S	A	V	I
L	S	J	E	L	N	O	I	T	A	C	A	V	S	P

AUGUST	OUTDOOR	PARK	LEMONADE
BASEBALL	FISHING	FUN	HEAT
HIKING	PICNIC	RECREATION	PLAY
INSECTS	JULY	JUNE	SOCCER
SOLSTICE	SPORTS	SUMMER	SUNSHINE
SWIM	TRAVEL	VACATION	WARM

Interest Inventory

Grade: _______ Name: _________________Date: _________________

If I could do anything I wanted to on the weekend , I would _______________

because ____.

If I could go anywhere in the world, I would want to go to ________________

because ____.

If I could study one subject all day long, it would be ______________________

because ____.

The subject I like least in school is _________________. I don't really like it

because ____.

The best book I ever read was ______________________________________.

I liked this book because ____.

My friend(s) is/are____.

If I Were in Charge

If I were in charge of our classroom, there would be no ________________ or ________________________. The students in our class would never have to __________________________________ or ______________________________ , and the teacher would always ______________________________________.

If I were in charge of our classroom, the first thing I would do would be to ____.

Then, I would ____.

If I Ran the School

If I ran the school, I would ____.

I would make sure that our school had lots of ____________________________ and I would never ask the students to ______________________________.

If I ran the school, I would buy a ________________________________

so that the students would be able to ____________________________.

Three things that I would not do if I ran the school are:

1. ____,

2. ____,

3. ____.

???

Mystery Door

???

Cut the following sentences into strips and put them in envelopes on your classroom door. Students must answer the questions to gain entrance to the classroom. Or, put them in a hat for kids to answer when lining up or in that extra five minutes of class time!

???

Name one of the grade one teachers.

???

??

Name one of the grade three teachers.

??

??

Name one of the grade five teachers.

??

??

What is the name of our school secretary?

??

??

What is the name of our school librarian?

??

??

What is the name of our school custodian?

??

??

What is the name of our school principal?

??

??

How many students are in our class?

??

??

How many boys are there in our class?

??

??

How many girls are there in our class?

??

??

What is your favourite food?

??

??

What is your favourite sport?

??

??

What is your favourite dessert?

??

??

What is your favourite restaurant?

??

??

What is your favourite T.V. show?

??

??

What is your favourite game to play?

??

??

If you could have any pet in the world, what would it be?

??

??

If you could travel anywhere in the world, where would you go?

??

??

Where is the pencil sharpener in our classroom?

??

??

Where is the tissue kept?

??

??

Where in our classroom is the Helper Chart?

??

??

Where do we hand in finished work?

??

??

Where is our class schedule posted?

??

??

Where are homework assignments posted?

??

??

What was your favorite part of summer holidays?

??

create your own

??

create your own

??

??

create your own

??

??

create your own

??

Find Someone Who...

Find someone who can answer YES to one of these statements. Put his or her name beside the statements. You may only write a person's name ONCE on this sheet. Good luck and have fun!

Find someone who...

1. Is wearing something yellow. ____________________
2. Is wearing a watch.____________________
3. Has brown eyes. ____________________
4. Likes to go jogging. ____________________
5. Plays a musical instrument. ____________________
6. Likes doing jigsaw puzzles. ____________________
7. Eats Cheerios for breakfast. ____________________
8. Has a pet with four legs. ____________________
9. Can play soccer. ____________________
10. Has never swum in the ocean. ____________________
11. Thinks hot dogs are wonderful. ____________________
12. Can stand on his or her head. ____________________

Find A Classmate Who...

13. Has been to Disneyland. ____________________

14. Had a headache last week. ____________________

15. Is going shopping this weekend. ____________________

16, Is older than you are. ____________________

17. Has a first name that begins with the same letter as yours. ____________________

18. Loves to do homework. ____________________

19. Has met someone famous. ____________________

20. Has flown over the ocean ____________________

21. Has a pet. ____________________

22. Loves pepperoni and mushroom pizza. ____________________

23. Is afraid of mice. ____________________

24. Loves to sing in the shower. ____________________

25. Can type. ____________________

26. Walls to school. ____________________

27. Has more brothers than sisters. ____________________

28. Has freckles. ____________________

29. Has a birthday in May. ____________________

Shhh!Shhh!Shhh!Shhh!Shhh!Shhh!Shhh!Shhh!Shhh!Shhh!Shhh!Shhh!Shhh!Shhh!Shhh!Shhh!

Secret Student

Shhh!Shhh!Shhh!Shhh!Shhh!Shhh!Shhh!Shhh!Shhh!Shhh!Shhh!Shhh!Shhh!Shhh!Shhh!Shhh!

I am __________ years old.

My favorite food of all time is ____________________ .

My favorite sport is ____________________ .

My favorite subject in school is _________________ .

I have ______________ eyes.

I have ______________ hair.

My favorite thing to do in my spare time is _________________________.

I am a (boy/girl) ____________ .

WHO AM I?

Secret Student Name: ________________________

Shhh!Shhh!Shhh!Shhh!Shhh!Shhh!Shhh!Shhh!Shhh!Shhh!Shhh!Shhh!Shhh!Shhh!Shhh!Shhh!

Descriptive Adjectives

Build	Personality	Hair Color	Hairstyle	Face
slim	engaging	red	straight	round
medium-build	shy	black	wavy	square
short	charming	brown	curly	oval
tall	quiet	blonde	neat	heart-shaped
broad	calm	grey	pony-tail	pear-shaped
shoulders	nice	white	with braids	high
slight	funny	dark	long	cheekbones
	sophisticated	light	short	
Dress	polite		parted on	**Complexion**
conservative	talkative	**Eye Color**	the right	olive-skinned
fashionable	reserved	blue	with bangs	light-skinned
sporty	sparkling	green		dark-skinned
casual	cheerful	brown		suntanned
elegant	friendly	hazel		
well-dressed	reliable	gray		

Eyebrows	Eyelashes	Nose	Chin
thick	thick	straight	square
thin	thin	flat	prominent
dark	long	long	dimpled
fair	short		small
			pointed

		FREE		

Something in Common

Name	In Common

Human Bingo

Likes chocolate	Wears glasses	Has a dog	Stays for lunch	Plays baseball
Plays soccer	Loves juice	Plays the piano	Gets up at 6:30	Has never had a filling
Has a pet fish	Has been to Hawaii	FREE	Has a little brother	Has green eyes
Loves math	Is a good skiier	Had cereal for breakfast	Has seen the ocean	Loves tacos
Can stand on their head	Loves to read	Has moved before	Is taller than you	Has their ears pierced

Biopoem Template

Line #1: First name only.

____

Line #2:Four traits that describe you.

_______________ _______________ _______________ _______________

Line #3: Sibling of/Son or Daughter of....

____

Line#4: Lover of (3 people or ideas)....

_______________ ____________________ __________________

Line #5: Who feels (3 things)....

_______________ ____________________ __________________

Line #6: Who needs (3 things)...

_______________ ____________________ __________________

Line #7: Who gives (3 things)...

_______________ ____________________ __________________

Line #8: Who fears (3 things)...

_______________ ____________________ __________________

Line #9: Who would like to see (3 places/things)...

_______________ ____________________ __________________

Line #10: Resident of (town/city)... ______________________

Line #11: Your last name only. _________________

Sample Completed Biopoem

Lori
Enthusiastic, outgoing, adventurous, cheerful
Sibling of Chris, Daughter of Larry and Jo-Anne
Lover of puppies, travel, and smiles
Who feels spontaneous, passionate, and spirited
Who needs activity, challenges, and fun
Who gives encouragement, hugs, and smiles
Who fears becoming complacent, taking those I love for granted, and mistreatment of animals
Who would like to see Africa, South America, and India
Resident of Edmonton
Friesen

Special Class Project: Time Capsules!

Monday, September 10, 2007

Dear Parents,

Our class is about to embark on a very special activity to celebrate the beginning of a brand new school year and we need your help! We are going to be making our very own time capsules. For this activity, your child will need to bring the following activities to school by **Monday, September 24th**.

In a plastic bag clearly labelled with your child's name, please send:

1.An EMPTY paper towel role.
2.Five small objects or photos which represent your child, and which can fit inside of the paper towel role. These items can be objects such as magazine photos of your child's favourite foods, games, activities, sports, or hobbies, or photos of your child's best friends, relatives, and/or pets. Please feel free to include small items as well, such as a medal earned or a small toy or action figure. The items selected should represent your child's favourite things and/or accomplishments at this time in his or her life.

Your child will receive all of these items back in their time capsule at the end of the year, and will be carefully cared for by myself until this time. Thank you very much for your assistance with this very special project!

Sincerely,

Mrs. Lori Friesen

Time Capsule Activity:

My Favourite Things!

By: ____________________

Date: ____________________

My Favourite Food	My Favourite Hobby
My Best Friends	**My Favourite ____________________**

Mandala Poem Sample

I am like an owl,
Wise, smart, and quiet.
I am not a pig,
Loud, messy, and crude.
I am yellow,
Smart, logical, and friendly.
I am not black,
Intimidating and closed-minded.
I am a sports car,
Fast, shiny, and new.
I am not a truck,
Loud, heavy, and menacing.
I am sunshine,
Shiny, sparkling, and beautiful.

I am like a ______________________;
(animal)

______________, ______________, and ______________.

I am not a ______________________;
(animal)

__________________ and __________________.

I am like ______________________;
(colour)

______________, ______________, and ______________.

I am not ______________________;
(colour)

__________________ and __________________.

I am like a ______________________;
(vehicle)

______________, ______________, and ______________.

I am not a ______________________;
(vehicle)

__________________ and __________________.

I am ______________________;
(weather)

______________, ______________, and ______________.

Written By: ______________________

My Mandala

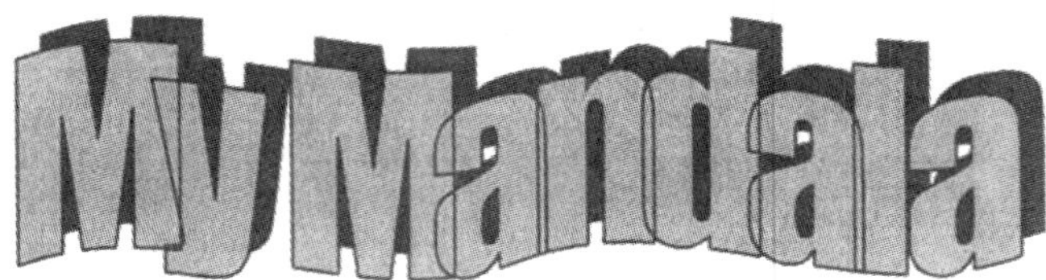

Template #1

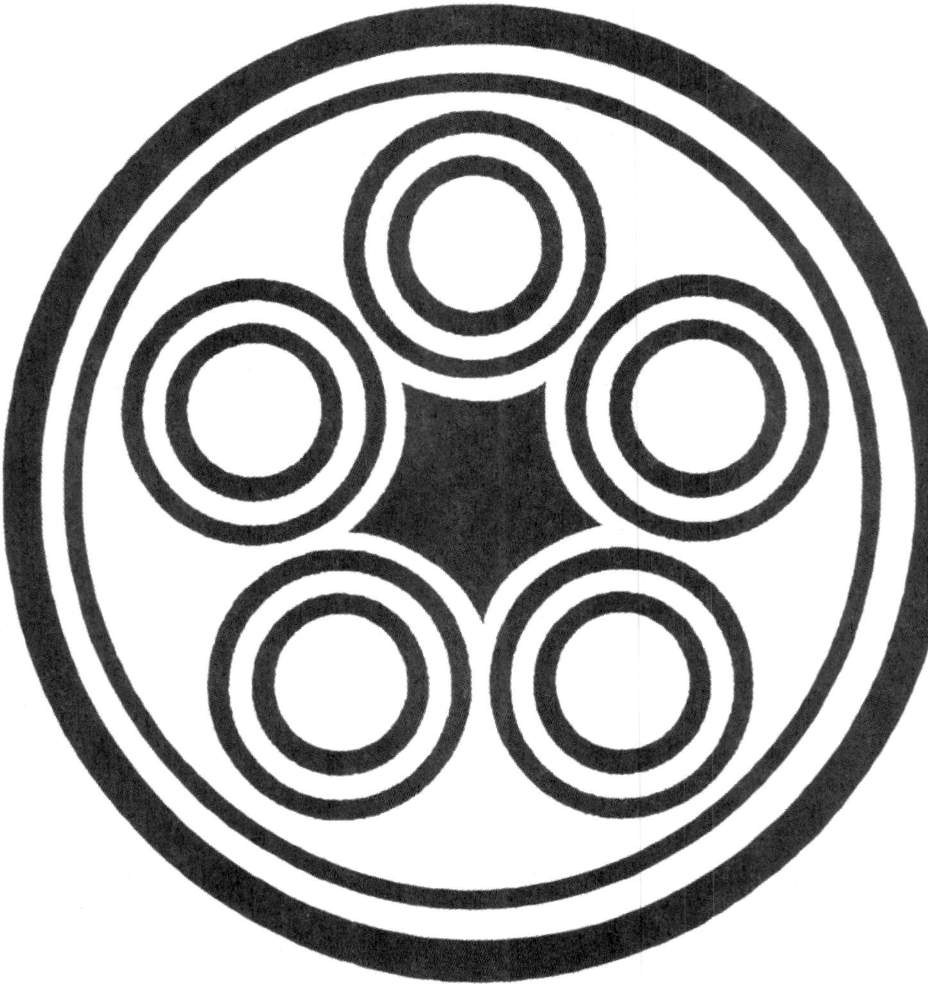

* To be illustrated by the student using pictures from their poem, cut out, and mounted onto a large sheet of paper to be displayed above their poem.

Template #2

Template #3

Parent Letter: Personal Presentations!

Each Friday we will be celebrating the life of one of our classmates. On this day, your child will be able to share and tell about his/her family, special traditions, favourites (foods, colour, movie, etc.) with his/her parent for the class. (Please see the sign-up sheet below to select a day that would be suitable for you). It is the responsibility of the special student to also provide a snack of his/her choice for the class to be enjoyed following their presentation.

Your child will be presenting after the morning recess, from approximately 11:15 - 11:25 a.m., and the class will then ask questions about their presentation. Then, the students in our class will write three sentences about what we learned about our classmate that day. Finally, we will enjoy a light snack provided by the special student. We will be finished shortly before dismissal at 11:45 a.m.

To help your child to present, I recommend using a large piece of bristle board to mount pictures of family, favourites, and significant events and/or successes your child has achieved outside of school. (I can provide paper for you upon request!) You can take this poster back home with you immediately following your child's presentation.

I will send home a reminder with your child one week before his or her Personal Presentation is scheduled. I look forward to seeing you on your child's special day!

Sincerely,

Lori Friesen

Personal Presentation Sign-Up Sheet

Date	Name of Child	Name of Parent and Phone Number
Sept. ____	____________________	______________________________
Sept. ____	____________________	______________________________
Sept. ____	____________________	______________________________
Oct. ____	____________________	______________________________
Oct. ____	____________________	______________________________
Oct. ____	____________________	______________________________
Oct. ____	____________________	______________________________
Nov. ____	____________________	______________________________
Nov. ____	____________________	______________________________
Nov. ____	____________________	______________________________
Nov. ____	____________________	______________________________
Dec. ____	____________________	______________________________
Dec. ____	____________________	______________________________
Jan. ____	____________________	______________________________
Jan. ____	____________________	______________________________
Jan. ____	____________________	______________________________
Jan. ____	____________________	______________________________

Date	Name of Child	Name of Parent and Phone Number
Feb. ____	____________________	______________________________
Feb. ____	____________________	______________________________
Feb. ____	____________________	______________________________
Feb. ____	____________________	______________________________
Mar. ____	____________________	______________________________
Mar. ____	____________________	______________________________
Mar. ____	____________________	______________________________
Mar. ____	____________________	______________________________
April ____	____________________	______________________________
April ____	____________________	______________________________
April ____	____________________	______________________________
April ____	____________________	______________________________
April ____	____________________	______________________________
May ____	____________________	______________________________
May ____	____________________	______________________________
May ____	____________________	______________________________
May ____	____________________	______________________________
June ____	____________________	______________________________
June ____	____________________	______________________________
June ____	____________________	______________________________

Personal Presentation Reminder!

Dear ______________________________ ,

This is just a short note to remind you that your child's Personal Presentation is on ______________________________ .

Your child will be presenting from approximately 11:15 to - 11:25 a.m., after which we will ask questions about their presentation. Then, the students in our class will write three sentences about what we learned about our special classmate that day. Finally, please don't forget to provide a light snack for your child to share with his/her classmates after the presentation! We will be finished shortly before dismissal at 11:45 a.m.

To help your child to present, I recommend using a large piece of bristle board to mount pictures of family, favourites (foods, activities, cartoons, etc.), and significant events and/or successes your child has achieved outside of school. Because pictures and mementos are invaluable, I ask that you take all materials home with you following your child's presentation. Thank you very much in advance for your time and participation. Please don't hesitate to call me should you have any further questions!

Sincerely,

Lori Friesen

Dear Parent,

We will be doing a special cooking project on ____________________ in the morning. Please send ____________________________________ with your child ________________________ on this day. Thank you very much!

Sincerely,

Lori Friesen

Dear Parent,

We will be doing a special cooking project on ____________________ in the morning. Please send ____________________________________ with your child ________________________ on this day. Thank you very much!

Sincerely,

Lori Friesen

Special Cooking Project!

____

Ingredients:

______________________ ______________________

______________________ ______________________

______________________ ______________________

______________________ ______________________

Directions:

1. ______________________________
2. ______________________________
3. ______________________________
4. ______________________________
5. ______________________________
6. ______________________________
7. ______________________________
8. ______________________________

Insert photo here

My

Grade ___________

Memory Book!

Year: __________

____

Elementary School

My Memory Book

Swimming With Our Class!

My Memory Book

For our class Christmas party this year, we__________________

and we __________________________. My Secret Santa was

__________________ . He/She gave me ________________________.

I think that the best thing about Christmas is ______________.

During the Christmas holidays, I ______________________________.

The one thing that I will remember the most about Christmas this

year is ____.

My Easter Vacation

My Memory Book

Random Acts of Kindness Week

My Memory Book......

Three random acts of kindness that I have done for others this week are:

____

____

____

Three random acts of kindness that have been done for me this week are:

____

____

____

Substitute Teacher Information

Thank you very much for coming in today! Here is some information you should know:
You will find a copy of our timetable and a class list in this folder for your use.

Attendance: The office will give you an attendance sheet. Please send this back to the office with one of the students once you have taken attendance. If no attendance sheet is provided, please use one of the class lists provided in this folder.

Name Tags: These are in a wooden box on the top of my filing cabinet.

Morning Routine: The students have 'Morning Message' books. They are to (try) to write the message on the whiteboard, filling all of the blanks in their books. If there is not a message on the board from me, please write one introducing yourself; I usually put blanks where the vowels are, unless it's a very difficult word. Please also include the complete date. We then go over it as a class, and the children hand in their completed books on the white shelf at the back for marking. They get a small sticker for no (or very few) errors. **Once at least half of the class has finished their morning warm up, invite the children into the reading corner for calendar time.** If it is at least October, I choose the person who has been following directions and who has walked quietly to the reading corner to lead calendar time for us (otherwise I do calendar myself in September!). Topics we need to cover include:

- Putting the current date on the calendar
- Changing the number of school days
- Changing the temperature (high) for the day
- Leading the class in the weekly poem using the pointer stick

I then take over to lead a short discussion regarding days of school we've had in relation to money. For example, if there have been 76 days of school, I challenge the children to tell me how we could make up that number using a variety of different coins. I.e.) 2 quarters, 2 dimes, a nickel and a penny, etc. You can use the money in the pocket chart to make several different combinations with the students.

After Lunch Routine: As soon as the students arrive after lunch, they are to write the information on the white-board in their agenda books. Then, I go around and check all of their books. **Please initial beside yesterday's date to acknowledge that you have seen their books and any notes the parents have written.**

Behaviour Programs:
If there are children who break our class rules, I print their name up on the board as a warning. The second time the behaviour occurs, they receive a checkmark beside their name. This means that they will need to stay in for recess to talk with me about it. Two checkmarks (rare, but it happens...) requires a phone call home to mom and dad.

Discipline Guidelines:
There is a treasure map on the blackboard in the reading corner. The children are able to earn **one or two steps on the treasure map for following the class rules** (posted on the side blackboard). When the students reach the end of the map, the children have earned a popcorn party! Alternatively, the children can lose spaces on the map for not following directions/listening etc.

Home Reading Routine:
The children exchange their home reading books only once per week. Each Thursday morning, **Mrs.** ___________ comes in to exchange the books for me. She is wonderful and knows exactly what to do! Please have the children bring their home reading book bags to the large back table, and she will return the previously read books to the shelf and then re-assign this weeks' books.

Classroom Assistant: ___________ is our classroom assistant, and she is assigned to work specifically with _____________. _____________ follows an independent program for language arts and for math, and does her stretches in our classroom during gym time. Other than these subjects, she participates fully in the regular routines and lessons of our classroom, with her assistant adapting any assignments not appropriate for her.

Classroom Parent Volunteers: I am very fortunate to have such a strong support network of parents who volunteer in my classroom on a regular basis. There is a schedule on the side of my filing cabinet indicating who will be coming and when each day of the week. They usually have a job to do and already know what it is! If not, they know where I keep all of my wonderful little parent help projects (by the frog bulletin board…)

Library Procedures:
The children have two books each from the library. All books they have signed out are listed on the sheet from the librarian (either in my mailbox in the office or on my desk). Please do a quick check that everyone has his or her books before leaving for the library. When they get into the library, they are to return their books in the return slot on their way in. Then, our librarian _______________ usually reads them a story in the viewing area of the library. The children are then welcome to choose **one fiction and one non-fiction** book from the library. Please ensure the children use the book paddles to keep their place when selecting books. When the

majority of the students have selected and signed out books, they line up single file before returning to the classroom. **If everyone in our class has returned their books, our class receives an 'apple' with our name on it to be put on the library bulletin board.** This is important to the children, as the "No Overdue Champs" class (the class with not overdue books) receives donuts at the end of the month from the library! When we return from the library the students need to print the titles of the two books they have just taken out in their Home Reading notebooks (in their blue denim home reading bags), and then put their books/bags on their hook, ready to go home.

<u>**Computer Procedure:**</u>
________________ is our computer specialist, and he is most often in the computer lab when we arrive for our scheduled computer time to answer any questions or help you out in any way! The children have pre-assigned seats in the lab (there is a seating arrangement included in this little package). The children are to first come and sit down by the large screen computer for a short lesson prior to their individual computer time; once they go to their computers, they are not to be getting up and walking around the lab unless in need of assistance, and the noise level needs to be kept low in respect for other classes in the library at this time.

<u>**Gym Procedures:**</u>
Before going to gym, the children line up single file in our classroom and I select two students who get to help with equipment (setting up and putting away) for that day. Once we get into the gym, the students usually do 3 laps around the gym (while we set up any needed equipment) and then meet me in the centre circle. Then, please follow the lesson provided. Throughout the class I am watching for 2 "Stars" - children who are following directions, displaying good sportsmanship, and respecting their class/team mates. At the end of the class, I have the girls and the boys line up in two different lines. I select the two stars for the day (one boy and one girl), and we give each a round of applause. Those children then get to go for a drink first. After getting a drink, we wait on the bench in the boot room and then head back to our classroom.

<u>**Brown Slips:**</u>
This is a school-wide initiative to reward children for outstanding behaviour. They are simply slips of tan paper (in the paper holder on my desk - the children will show you), on which the students' full name and grade are printed, along with the reason for receiving the brown slip. This can be anything from being kind to another student, being a good listener, being courteous, or getting 100% on a difficult test. The child then takes the brown slip down to the office where they put it in the cardboard school bus. Draws are made in the office once a week for various prizes and rewards, and selected students are then called down to the office over the intercom to receive their reward during morning announcements. The children LOVE these, and they are a great way to reinforce positive behaviour. You are welcome to use these brown slips as a positive reinforcement.

Fire Drill Procedure: There is a fire drill folder on the brown shelf by the door, and our fire escape route is posted on the wall. The last child out of the room needs to turn off the lights and shut the door. Please count to ensure that we have all of the children, and then send 2 students with that number for our class to 'the shed' on the east side of the school. The secretary will be there to meet them and take our class count. When the kids arrive back with the group and the alarm is turned off, we can then go back into the school.

Lock-Down Procedure: This is posted on the wall by the phone.

Pull-Out Programs:
_____________ is our Early Literacy language specialist. She will pull out the following children throughout the day (in the afternoon) to work on literacy skills: ___________________, ___________________, and __________________.
We have __ children receiving help with speech at this time from _____________, our Speech Language Pathologist: __________________ and ______________________.

Early Finishers:
If children are finished their work before others in the class, they are welcome to use the "Mind Candy" centre (on the side bulletin board), which is loaded with enrichment activities, read a book silently at their desk or in the reading corner, doodle in their purple books at their desks, or 'make a cartoon' with the cartoon books on the shelves under the student mailboxes.

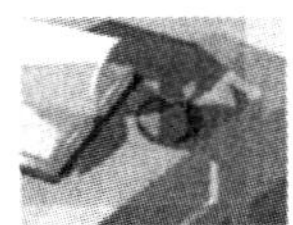

Lesson Plan Template

Subject: ______________________ Grade Level: ____________

Number of Minutes: ______________ Date: __________________

Objective:
Materials:
Procedure:
Evaluation:
Teacher Notes/Reflection:

Sample Day Plan Template

	Date:
8:25-9:00	
9:00-9:30	
9:30-10:00	
10:00-10:15	Recess
10:15-10:45	
10:45-11:15	
11:15-11:45	

12:45- 1:15	
1:15- 1:45	
1:45- 2:15	
2:15- 2:25	Recess
2:30- 3:00	
3:00- 3:30	

<u>Supervision Duties:</u>

<u>Important Meetings/Things to Remember:</u>

Sample Weekly Plan Template

	Monday	Tuesday	Wednesday	Thursday	Friday
8:30 - 9:00					
9:00 - 9:30					
9:30 - 10:00					
10:00 - 10:15	Recess	Recess	Recess	Recess	Recess
10:15 - 10:45					
10:45 - 11:15					
11:15 - 11:45					
11:45 - 12:45	Lunch	Lunch	Lunch	Lunch	Lunch
12:45 - 1:15					
1:15 - 1:45					
1:45 - 2:15					
2:15 - 2:30	Recess	Recess	Recess	Recess	Recess
2:30 - 3:00					
3:00 - 3:30					

Sample Completed Week Plan

Mrs. Friesen	Monday	Tuesday	Wednesday	Thursday	Friday
8:30 - 9:00	Language Arts Home/School Journal	Writer's Workshop	Reading	Writer's Workshop	Computers
9:00 - 9:30	Music (Ms. Fender)	Writer's Workshop	Reading	Writer's Workshop	Home/School Journal
9:30 - 10:15	Library U.S.S.R.	Spelling/Printing U.S.S.R.	Reading U.S.S.R.	Spelling/Printing U.S.S.R.	Music (Ms. Fender)
10:15 - 10:30	Recess	Recess	Recess	Recess	Recess
10:30 - 10:45	Reading	Math	Math	Reading	U.S.S.R.
10:45 - 11:15	Phys. Ed. (Mr. Scott)	Math	Math	Music (Ms. Fender)	Personal Presentation
11:15 - 11:45	Language Arts	Math	Math	Health	Personal Presentation
11:45 - 12:45	Noon Hour	Noon Hour	Noon Hour	Noon Hour	
12:45 - 1:15	Math (Exploration Centres)	Computers	Health	Computers (Mr. Scott)	
1:15 - 1:45	Math (Exploration Centres)	Phys. Ed.	Phys. Ed. (Mr. Scott)	Science	
1:45 - 2:15	Science	Science	Science	Science	
2:15 - 2:25	Recess	Recess	Recess	Recess	
2:25 - 3:00	Social Studies	Art	Social Studies	Social Studies	
3:00 - 3:30	Viewing (Mr. Scott)	Art	Social Studies	Social Studies	

Year Plan Template

Subject	September	October	November	December	January
Language Learning					
Math					
Social Studies					
Science					
Phys. Ed					
Art					
Music					
Health					

Year Plan Template Cont'd...

Subject	January	March	April	May	June
Language Learning					
Math					
Social Studies					
Science					
Phys. Ed					
Art					
Music					
Health					

Special Person Award

Thank you for all of your hard work. You are a SUPER kid!

Trade this coupon in for a special treat!

Special Person Award

Thank you for all of your hard work. You are a SUPER kid!

Trade this coupon in for a special treat!

Special Person Award

Thank you for all of your hard work. You are a SUPER kid!

Trade this coupon in for a special treat!

Special Person Award

Thank you for all of your hard work. You are a SUPER kid!

Trade this coupon in for a special treat!

Special Person Award

Thank you for all of your hard work. You are a SUPER kid!

Trade this coupon in for a special treat!

Special Person Award

Thank you for all of your hard work. You are a SUPER kid!

Trade this coupon in for a special treat!

This award goes to

____

For

____

Congratulations!

You are such a special kid!
I am very proud of you for all of your hard work.
Thank you for being you ☺

To: ____________________________

Love, ____________________________

Congratulations!

You have earned this certificate
For your excellent behaviour in class.
Keep up the great work!
Love, ____________________________

You are a Star!

All-Star Student Award!

CONGRATULATIONS __________________
YOU HAVE EARNED THIS SPECIAL AWARD
FOR DOING YOUR VERY BEST IN CLASS.
YOU ARE A STAR!

Exemplary Acts of Kindness

This certificate is awarded to

____

For Displaying Exemplary Acts of Kindness
Towards their Classmates

Date: __________________

School: ____________________________

Signed: __________________

Three C Award

**For Demonstrating
Strength of Character,
Consideration, and
Caring
In Our Classroom**

Year: ______________________

School: ______________________

Signed: ______________________
Teacher

Sample Meet the Teacher Night Parent Letter

Monday, September 9, 2002

Dear Parents,

In preparation for our school Open House tomorrow evening, I wanted to inform you of sign-ups for various activities in our classroom this year. If you will be unable to attend our Open House but would like to volunteer for some of the following events/activities, please include a note in your child's communication book indicating how you would like to help out, and I will confirm by writing back to you. I can't thank you enough in advance for all of your support and dedication!

Regular Classroom Helpers
If you would like to help out in our classroom on a regular basis to assist with the preparation of instructional materials, work with individual or small groups of children, and read with children one-on-one, please let me know what day(s) would suit you. This could be a commitment of one hour/morning/afternoon each week or every two weeks.

Special Occasions
Please let me know if you would like to volunteer to bring/send cookies or cupcakes on Halloween, Christmas, Valentine's Day, The 100th Day of School, Easter, or at the End-of-the-Year party, or if you would be willing to pop some popcorn should our class earn this reward! I will send a reminder home closer to the event, as these dates are not yet set.

Scholastic Book Orders
I am looking for a parent who would be willing to set aside approximately a one-hour time commitment each month to put together and send our

Scholastic book orders for our class. I will send out the initial notices each month and collect the orders/money from the children; your responsibility would be to simply place our order.

Donations for our Class Auctions

I will be holding two class auctions this year. The first will be at the end of January and the second at the end of June. During these auctions, the children will be able to spend the "money" they have earned from bringing their communication books to and from school on a regular basis. This is a very valuable activity as it teaches children money skills while they earn positive rewards for being responsible. While on your travels to the dollar store or book store, should you find an item or items you would like to donate to our class auction simply send it to school with your child, and I will collect and keep all items until January. We will then begin a second collection for the end of June. I believe this will prove to be a fun and worthwhile activity, and one that the children are really looking forward to!

Field Trips/Special Events

As field trips and other special events come up I will send home notices explaining the details of the events and requests for parent drivers at that time. Possible field trips/events for this year are listed below, with confirmed dates in bold:

September 20	**Class Pictures**
September 26	**Book Fair**
October 1	**Afer-School Skating begins**
October	Recycling Plant/Waste Treatment Plant field trip to supplement our science unit on "Waste in Our World" (yes, the kids are really excited about this one - ha ha).
November	Safety City Presentation on Bullying
December 17	**Christmas at the Fort**
December	Swimming at Nicholas Sheran
January 30	**Class Auction**
February 27-28	**Book Fair**
February	Safety City Presentation on Internet Safety
February	Galt Museum Field Trip: Making Do or Doing Without (The Great Depression)

March	Safety City Presentation on Outdoor Play
April 28-May 2	**Trickster (Professional Drama Company)**
May	Bicycle Safety field trip to Safety City
May	Field Trip to Head-Smashed-In-Buffalo-Jump
June	Second Class Auction

Just a reminder that our Open House begins tomorrow evening with a general introduction to the staff at 7:00 p.m. in the gym, individual classroom sessions at 7:15, and the slide show in the gym at 7:45.

I am looking forward to an exciting and rewarding year, and I hope to see you tomorrow evening!

Sincerely,

Mrs. Lori Friesen

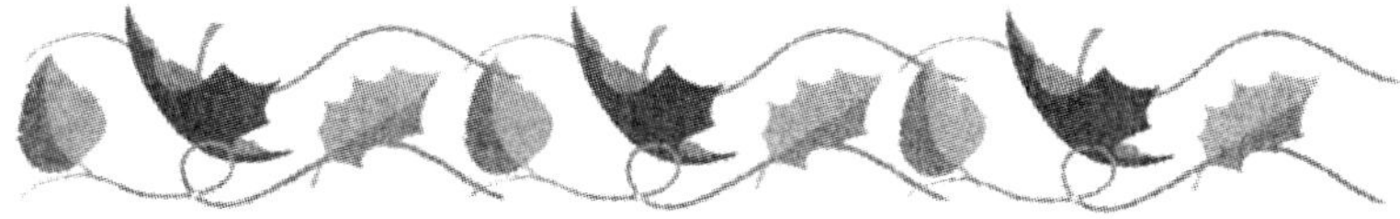

Parent Volunteer Sign-Up Sheet

Halloween

Fruit and/or vegetables with dip ______________________

Cheese and crackers ______________________

Cookies, cupcakes, or muffins ______________________

Drinks and napkins ______________________

Christmas

Fruit and/or vegetables with dip ______________________

Cheese and crackers ______________________

Cookies, cupcakes, or muffins ______________________

Drinks and napkins ______________________

Valentine's Day

Fruit and/or vegetables with dip ______________________

Cheese and crackers ______________________

Cookies, cupcakes, or muffins ______________________

Drinks and napkins ______________________

100th Day of School

Fruit and/or vegetables with dip ______________________

Cheese and crackers ______________________

Cookies, cupcakes, or muffins ______________________

Drinks and napkins ______________________

Easter

Fruit and/or vegetables with dip ______________________

Cheese and crackers ______________________

Cookies, cupcakes, or muffins ______________________

Drinks and napkins ______________________

Last Day of School

Fruit and/or vegetables with dip ______________________

Cheese and crackers ______________________

Cookies, cupcakes, or muffins ______________________

Drinks and napkins ______________________

Compliments of Ms. Elizabeth Nevels, Grade 2 Teacher

I would like to volunteer to pop popcorn for a class popcorn party should our class earn this reward!

Parent Name	Student Name	Phone Number
1.		
2.		
3.		
4.		
5.		
6.		
7.		
8.		

Dear Parents,

The students in our class have been working very hard for the past two and a half months to learn school and class rules, follow directions in class, and be caring citizens in our classroom community. Therefore, we have earned our very first popcorn party to reward our efforts! I would like to invite the children to come to school dressed in their PJ's on ______________________ as part of this celebration. They are welcome to bring with them one small stuffed animal (no larger than their forearm, please!) and a pillow with which to snuggle during this celebration. **If you would be willing to help at home by popping popcorn for part of our class, please write me a short note in your child's agenda!** Please take a moment to tell your child how proud you are of them – we are off to a wonderful start in grade two!

Sincerely,
Lori Friesen

Dear Parents,

The students in our class have been working very hard for the past two and a half months to learn school and class rules, follow directions in class, and be caring citizens in our classroom community. Therefore, we have earned our very first popcorn party to reward our efforts! I would like to invite the children to come to school dressed in their PJ's on ______________________ as part of this celebration. They are welcome to bring with them one small stuffed animal (no larger than their forearm, please!) and a pillow with which to snuggle during this celebration. **If you would be willing to help at home by popping popcorn for part of our class, please write me a short note in your child's agenda!** Please take a moment to tell your child how proud you are of them – we are off to a wonderful start in grade two!

Sincerely,
Lori Friesen

Assessment Portfolio

Dear Parents,

I will be sending home all tests and major assignments in this envelope for your perusal. Please go through the tests/assignments with your child, and then send them back to school in this envelope after signing and dating this sheet. Thank you!

Description of Test or Assignment	Date Returned to School	Parent Signature

Description of Test or Assignment	Date Returned to School	Parent Signature

September 4, 2002

Dear Grade 4 Parents,

This year, I would like to try something new to improve my communication with you, the parents. It is called "The Communication Book." Very often, it is difficult to touch base by phone to keep you up to date due to both yours and my own busy schedule. This doesn't mean that I don't welcome your phone calls , particularly about 'delicate' issues, but that I can better keep you informed about the daily events in our classroom by using your child's Communication Book.

This is how I would like the program to work. Each morning, as the children come in for the day,they will bring their Communication Book. They will place it on one corner of their desk. As I begin the day, I will check each book for a parent's initial or signature (whatever you are comfortable with). If there are announcements or upcoming events that I would like you to know about, the children will spend a few minutes and write these into their Communication Books. If you have a written message to the teacher, these books will be collected and at some point in the day a note will be written back to you. It would also be a convenient place for you to tell me about doctor or dentist appointments, or other events that might keep your child out of school.

These Communication Books will also be a place where your child will write down their homework assignments each day. This way, you will be informed about the work that is due or in some cases overdue.

On occasion, I may need to inform you about a behaviour issue concerning your child. I will only mention the incident in the communication book. If the concern is of a more serious nature, I will contact you by telephone. If you need more details, I would welcome a telephone call.

I am just initiating this process for the first time and would appreciate your feedback as we go through the year. I would like to thank you for taking the time to ask for the Communication Book each evening, if it isn't offered to you. I have talked to the children and have asked that they don't pull this book out of their backpack just as you are heading out the door to work or school in the morning, but that they talk to you and decide how you would like to handle the process at home. I hope that it will become a routine that takes very little time to complete each day, so that it isn't a burden to your family.

At the end of each week, if your child has earned a minimum of four initials by both you and myself, (s)he will be given one 'Scholar Dollar' to spend at our class auction in January. I am in the process of collecting small items that will be 'up for bid' for our auction over the next several months. If you would like to donate any items for our auction, please send them to school with your child and I will keep them in a safe place until our auction in January. Popular items include small stuffed animals, gel pens, markers and other art materials, sunglasses, and 'surprise bags.'

Finally, I would like to thank you in advance for your help in making this project a success, and most of all for helping me to better communicate your child's progress and successes this year.

Sincerely,

Ms. A. Grant

Our Class Auction!

My name is ____________________

Before Our Auction

I have earned ______ scholar dollars to spend at our auction.
I am planning to bid on these items:

1. ____

2. ____

3. ____

After Our Auction

I have ______ scholar dollars left after our auction.
I bought these items:

1. ____

2. ____

3. ____

Our Class Auction!

Student Name	Item Purchased	Cost

Class Auction Gift Certificates

Gift Certificate

Class Auction

This certificate entitles you to:

Congratulations!

Not redeemable for cash. Prize value: Priceless

Gift Certificate

Class Auction

This certificate entitles you to:

Congratulations!

Not redeemable for cash. Prize value: Priceless

Just a little note of thanks
For your support with our
"Class Auction!"

It was a huge success thanks to your generous donations!

Sincerely,

____

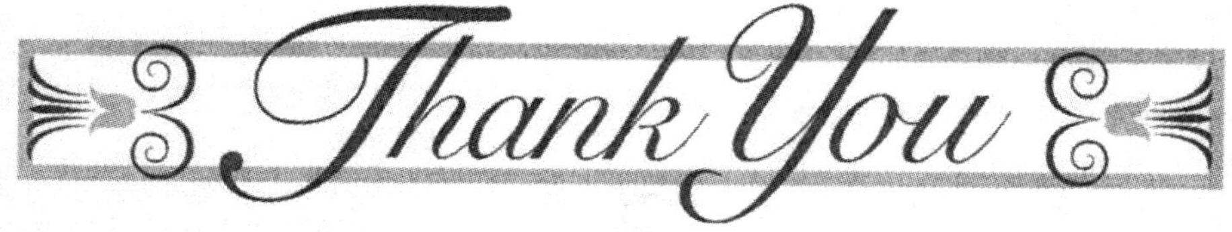

Just a little note of thanks
For your support with our
"Class Auction!"

It was a huge success thanks to your generous donations!

Sincerely,

____

Individual Student Sticker or Stamp Charts

Student Name: ______________________

Objective: __________________________

Student Name: ______________________

Objective: __________________________

☺ Report Card Comments for ____________________

Personal Growth
Work Habits
Reading Comprehension Fluency
Writing Content Organization Conventions Writing/Printing
Math Basic Skills Problem Solving Communicates Math. Thinking
Science Social Studies
Other:
Term Goal #1:
Term Goal #2:
Parent Concerns: Follow-Up:

Letter to Next Year's Class

______________, ________, 200___

Dear ________________ Grader,

Welcome to Grade _____! You are probably feeling a little bit nervous right now. Don't worry, Ms. _____________ will help you as much as she can. Here are three things I have learned in this grade that will help you out a lot:

1.____

2.____

3.____

One of the things I liked the most about being in this classroom was __________________________________. I really liked this because ________________________. My favourite subject in this grade was _____________ because we got to learn about ____________________. I know that you'll have a great year!

Sincerely,

____

Book Talks

You will have one week to prepare for your book talk. Please make sure that you have filled in all of the information on this sheet, and hand it in following your book talk. Good luck and have fun!

Student Name: ______________________________
Date of Book Talk: ___________________________
Title of Book: ______________________________
Book Author: _______________________________

A. Think about questions you would like to ask the class about your book. Here are some ideas to get you started:

Before you read, you could ask a question about the book cover, the author, or about how many people have read the book. You might want to ask how many people in our class like this book.
While you read, you may want to ask questions like: Would you ever do this? I wonder why... ? Do you know anyone like this character?
When you are finished reading, you may want to ask a question about what the class thinks will happen next, whether or not the liked the book, or if they would read this book on their own.

Your own questions:
1.______________________________________
2.______________________________________
3.______________________________________

B. Tell about why you chose this book to read to the class:
____
____
____
____
____
____

BOOKMARKS

Never Forget...
(Insert text here)
Grade _____
Class of _______

Never Forget...
(Insert text here)
Grade _____
Class of _______

100 Ways You Are Wonderful

You are so special! - How Extraordinary! – Far Out- Great!- Outstanding Performance- Marvelous- I Can't Get Over It! – Wonderful- Amazing Effort!- Unbelievable Work!- Your Work Is Out Of Sight- Phenomenal!- You've Got It- Superb!- You're Special- Cool!- Excellent-Your Project Is 1st Rate!- Way To Go!- You've Outdone Yourself- Thumbs Up!- What A Great Listener- Your Help Counts- You Came Through- Terrific!- You Tried Hard- Fabulous- You Made It Happen- You're A Real Trooper- It Couldn't Be Better!- The Time You Put In Really Shows- Bravo!- You're Unique- Exceptional!- Fantastic Work!- Breathtaking!- You're A Great Example For Others- Keep Up The Great Work- Awesome!- I Knew You Had It In You!- You're A Good Sport!- You Should Be Proud- What An Imagination!- It's Everything I Hoped For- Stupendous- You're Sensational- Very Good!- A+ Work- You Made The Difference- Good For You- Take A Bow- Super Job- How Thoughtful Of You- Nice Going- Class Act- Well Done- You're Inspiring- How Artistic- You Go The Extra Mile!- Hooray For You!- You're A Joy!- You're A Shining Star- You're Amazing!- What A Great Idea!- Great Answer- Extra Special Work- You Deserve A Hug- You're Getting Better- You're Tops!- You Figured It Out- You've Got What It Takes- You're Neat!- Spectacular Work- You're #1- Remarkable!- You're A Winner- Beautiful!- Clever- You're So Kind- Wow!- Magnificent!- You're Sharp- You're A-OK!- You've Made Progress- Brilliant!- Thanks For Helping- Thanks For Caring- Great Discovery- What A Genius!- You've Earned My Respect- You're A Pleasure To Know- You're Very Talented- How Original- Very Brave- Congratulations!- You're A Champ- You're Super- I'm Impressed!- You're The Greatest- I'm Proud Of You!- Right On!

100 Ways You Are Wonderful

You are so special! - How Extraordinary! – Far Out- Great!- Outstanding Performance- Marvelous- I Can't Get Over It! – Wonderful- Amazing Effort!- Unbelievable Work!- Your Work Is Out Of Sight- Phenomenal!- You've Got It- Superb!- You're Special- Cool!- Excellent-Your Project Is 1st Rate!- Way To Go!- You've Outdone Yourself- Thumbs Up!- What A Great Listener- Your Help Counts- You Came Through- Terrific!- You Tried Hard- Fabulous- You Made It Happen- You're A Real Trooper- It Couldn't Be Better!- The Time You Put In Really Shows- Bravo!- You're Unique- Exceptional!- Fantastic Work!- Breathtaking!- You're A Great Example For Others- Keep Up The Great Work- Awesome!- I Knew You Had It In You!- You're A Good Sport!- You Should Be Proud- What An Imagination!- It's Everything I Hoped For- Stupendous- You're Sensational- Very Good!- A+ Work- You Made The Difference- Good For You- Take A Bow- Super Job- How Thoughtful Of You- Nice Going- Class Act- Well Done- You're Inspiring- How Artistic- You Go The Extra Mile!- Hooray For You!- You're A Joy!- You're A Shining Star- You're Amazing!- What A Great Idea!- Great Answer- Extra Special Work- You Deserve A Hug- You're Getting Better- You're Tops!- You Figured It Out- You've Got What It Takes- You're Neat!- Spectacular Work- You're #1- Remarkable!- You're A Winner- Beautiful!- Clever- You're So Kind- Wow!- Magnificent!- You're Sharp- You're A-OK!- You've Made Progress- Brilliant!- Thanks For Helping- Thanks For Caring- Great Discovery- What A Genius!- You've Earned My Respect- You're A Pleasure To Know- You're Very Talented- How Original- Very Brave- Congratulations!- You're A Champ- You're Super- I'm Impressed!- You're The Greatest- I'm Proud Of You!- Right On!

Yearbook Page Cards

Humour: The funniest thing that happened this year!	Great Books: The best books that I read this year.	Friends: Some of my best friends this year.
The People: All about my classmates.....	"Time Stands Still" My favourites at this point in time.	Changes: Ways I have changed this year.
Our Classroom: A "Bird's Eye View" of our classroom.	Recess: What I love about our school playground.	Special Events: My favourite field trip this year.
Projects: Special occasions or projects I want to remember.	Subjects: The subject I enjoyed the most this year.	My Teacher: One thing I'll always remember about my teacher.

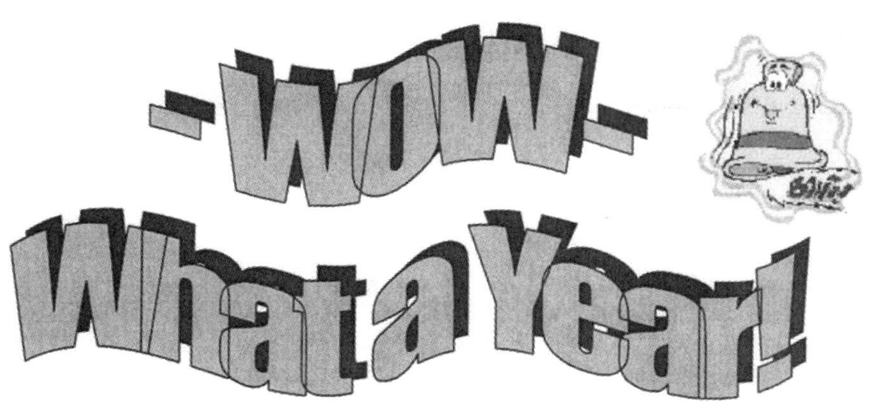

(Insert Photo Here)

Student Name: ______________________________

Teacher Name: _________________________

Grade: _______________

Date: _____________________________

School: ____

Class Yearbook Page

Think back on our year. What is one of the funniest things that happened this year?

Draw a picture to show what happened and then write one or two sentences to tell about it.

____

____

____

____

Class Yearbook Page

My Favourite Books

What are some of the best books you read this year?

In the space below, design a poster to advertise 1 or 2 books you love. Make sure you tell your audience what makes these books so special!

Book Title #1: ________________________________

Author: ________________________________

Book Title #2: ________________________________

Author: ________________________________

Class Yearbook Page

Who are some of your best friends this year? In the space below, either draw a picture of you and your friends doing something you love to do together, or draw something that reminds you of your friends. Then write one or two sentences telling about what makes your friend(s) special.

Class Yearbook Page

200__

My favorite movie is....
My favorite food is....
My favorite restaurant is....
My favorite TV show is....
My favorite thing to do is....
My favorite book is ....
My favorite song is ....
My favorite word is....

DREAMING OF THE FUTURE.....

Someday I hope to be a ....
Someday I hope to have a....
Someday I hope to go to ....

Class Yearbook Page

All About My Classmates

Working together with a partner, try to list at least one positive adjective to describe each of your classmates. Compare with other groups to see if you can add to your list!

Classmate's Name	Descriptors
1.	
2.	
3.	
4.	
5.	
6.	
7.	
8.	
9.	
10.	
11.	
12.	
13.	
14.	
15.	
16.	
17.	
18.	
19.	
20.	
21.	
22.	
23.	
24.	
25.	
26.	

Class Yearbook Page

This Year's Top Ten Events

In your opinion, what were the top ten highlights of this school year?

10.
9.
8.
7.
6.
5.
4.
3.
2.
1.

Class Yearbook Page

Class Yearbook Page

You Are So Special!!!

You are special. In the entire world there's nobody like you.

Since the beginning of time, there has never been another person like you. Nobody has your smile. Nobody has your eyes, your nose, your hair, and your voice. You're special.

No one can be found who has your printing. Nobody anywhere has your tastes- for food or music or art. No one sees things just as you do.

In all of time there's been no one who laughs like you. No one cries like you. No one reacts to any situation just as you would. You are special.

You are the only one in all of creation who has your set of abilities. Oh, there will always be somebody who is better at one of the things you are good at, but no one in the universe can reach the quality of your combination of talents, ideas, abilities, and feelings.

Through all of eternity no one will ever talk, walk, think, or do like you. You are rare. And in rarity there is great value.

Because of your great rare value, you need not attempt to imitate others. You will accept and celebrate your differences.

You are special. You are one of a kind. You are special!!!

Love,

____

You Are Worth

A MILLION...

To Me.
Love,

____

You Are Worth

A MILLION...

To Me.
Love,

____

End of the Year Gift: CD Cover Template

Grade Two Memories

Student Name:____________________

(Insert Photo Here)

Love,

____

200__

End of the Year Gift: CD Table of Contents Template

Table of Contents

1. First Day of Grade Two
2. Halloween
3. Treasure Chest and Map
4. Gingerbread Houses
5. Christmas
6. Penguins
6. Great Grade 2 Auction
7. 100th Day
8. Book Buddies
9. Helen Schuler
10. Valentine's Day
11. Easter
12. We Can Make a Difference
13. Fort Whoop-Up
14. Swimming

A Big Thumbs Up

to

____

For all of the time, effort and love you have brought to our classroom this year.

I am thankful to have had the opportunity to teach your child.
I appreciate you so very much!

Sincerely,

____

GENERAL-USE CHECKLISTS

I fill in one of these checklists with my students' names in alphabetical order at the beginning of the year and use them for everything from keeping track of who has brought back a Scholastic Book Order to who has received special awards and/or certificates in my classroom throughout the year. I have included several templates here for you to adapt for your own instructional needs.

STUDENT'S NAME	

STUDENT'S NAME		

STUDENT'S NAME	

Student's Name				

About the Author

Lori's experience within education is as extensive as her travel log. Having earned her certificate of English Language Training (CELTA) in Toronto, Lori began her career in E.S.L. as an assistant at the Lethbridge Community College in the Adult Language Centre. She completed her B.A./B.Ed. at the University of Lethbridge before leaving Canada to teach in Hong Kong and Japan. Afterwards, she traveled through Asia, Australia, New Zealand, Italy, and Germany.

Lori returned to Canada in order to complete her Masters in Education and wrote *The Handbook for Beginning Teachers of Elementary School* as the final project for her degree. Lori finished a course in Administrative Leadership Development in 2006 and capped off the experience by spending the summer in Italy and Greece where she completed the Creativity Workshop. She also taught elementary school for seven years for Lethbridge School District #51 and taught for one year in The Faculty of Education at the University of Lethbridge.

Currently, Lori is working towards earning her Ph.D. at the University of Alberta in the area of Language and Literacy in Elementary Education.